ON THE STUDY OF GREEK POETRY

SUNY Series, Intersections: Philosophy and Critical Theory
Rodolphe Gasché, editor

FRIEDRICH SCHLEGEL

ON THE STUDY OF GREEK POETRY

Translated, edited, and with a critical introduction by
Stuart Barnett

State University of New York Press

Published by
State University of New York Press, Albany

For information, address State University of New York Press
90 State Street, Suite 700, Albany, NY 12207

Production by Dana Foote
Marketing by Anne Valentine

Library of Congress Cataloging-in-Publication Data

Schlegel, Friedrich von, 1772–1829.
[Über das Studium der griechischen Poesie, 1795–1797. English]
On the study of Greek poetry / Friedrich Schlegel ; translated, edited,
and with a critical introduction by Stuart Barnett.
p. cm. — (SUNY series, Intersections)
Includes bibliographical references and index.
ISBN 0-7914-4829-0 (alk. paper) — ISBN 0-7914-4830-4 (pbk. : alk. paper)
1. Greek poetry—History and criticism. I. Barnett, Stuart, 1960– II. Title.
III. Intersections (Albany, N.Y.)

PA3093 .S3413 2001
881'.0109—dc21
00–048249

10 9 8 7 6 5 4 3 2 1

CONTENTS

ACKNOWLEDGMENTS

Acknowledgments are perhaps the most quintessentially Schlegelian moment of a book. They are the moment of parabasis, a suspension of presentation and argument, during which the audience—or, at least, *an* audience—is addressed directly. Schlegel reminds us that, far from being an aside, such gestures are fundamental to (and perhaps the ultimate purpose of) the drama of presentation. Thus, even though this is essentially not my presentation, I must indulge the desire to acknowledge the individuals and institutions that assisted this undertaking. I would like to thank: Patricia Festa Barnett, Benjamin Bennett, Peter Burgard, Emily Chasse, Rodolphe Gasché, Geoffrey Hartman, Charbra Jestin, Loftus Jestin, Winfried Menninghaus, Joan Packer, Alice Pentz, Johann Pillai, Karen Ritzenhoff, Sylvia Schmitz-Burgard, and Martha Wallach. I would also like to thank the interlibrary loan staff of the Burritt Library at Central Connecticut State University and the staff at the Avon Library. Central Connecticut State University generously supported this project with grants and release time; a Mellon Fellowship at Yale University provided a stimulating enivironment and access to materials.

A Note on the Translation

The basis of the present translation is the original edition of 1797. Schlegel subjected this study to extensive revision when it was republished in his collected works, *Friedrich Schlegels sämtliche Werke* (1822–1825). This edition is referred to in the text as W. I have provided translations in the notes of significant changes and alterations Schlegel made in the later edition as they do shed light on the text and the development of Schlegel's thought. However, the vast majority of these are minor word changes. I have decided not to make note of these. Noting all these changes would have increased the length of this volume by a half, making its apparatus cumbersome and confusing for the average reader. In addition, the changes often entail merely a slight shade of meaning, which would be virtually impossible to capture in translation. For purposes of comparison and reference, pagination is indicated for the two standard German editions of the essay: the *Kritische Friedrich Schlegel Ausgabe*, vol. I, Ernst Behler, ed. (Munich: Schöningh, 1958) and *Friedrich Schlegel, 1794–1802: Seine prosäische Jugendschriften,* ed. Jakob Minor (Vienna: Konegen, 1906). Page references to the Minor edition are indicated by the letter M.

Schlegel completed the text of the essay in 1795. It languished at the publisher for two years. When it was published in 1797, Schlegel wrote a preface to the essay that is, in fact, more of an afterword. It is included here in an appendix.

CRITICAL INTRODUCTION
THE AGE OF ROMANTICISM: SCHLEGEL FROM ANTIQUITY TO MODERNITY

> Friedrich Schlegel often remained
> incomprehensible even to his friends.
> —Walter Benjamin

It often comes as a surprise to learn that Friedrich Schlegel—who is widely understood to have been not only at the forefront of European Romanticism as one of its earliest practitioners but also at the forefront of the effort to provide Romanticism with its own aesthetics—was an ardent enthusiast of the classics. Indeed, his enthusiasm was such that even that representative of what came to be called German Classicism, Friedrich Schiller, was prompted to characterize it—albeit unfairly—as indicative of a "Graecomania."[1] The association at first seems so odd and uncharacteristic that it is very tempting to dismiss it as mere apprenticeship work on the part of a budding critic and artist. To do this, however, would be a grave mistake. For the mature work of Schlegel must remain to a great extent inexplicable if it is not foregrounded in this earlier period. This is because, simply put, the writings of the "classicist" Schlegel pose the question to which the writings of the Romantic Schlegel attempt to provide the answer.

In order to understand this seeming paradox, it is helpful to contextualize it with some brief biographical considerations. Schlegel was born on March 10, 1772 in Hannover. He was the youngest son in a family of seven children. Schlegel was a difficult, brooding child; yet he was fortunate to have had August Wilhelm for an older brother. Throughout his life, August Wilhelm served as both friend and mentor. At the age of fifteen, Schlegel was apprenticed to a banker in Leipzig. This soon proved to be thoroughly unsuitable for Schlegel and so, two years later in 1790, he joined August Wilhelm in Göttingen to study law. He moved a year later, however, to continue his study of the law in Leipzig. There he began the important friendship with Novalis. It did not take long for Schlegel to realize that literature was of far greater interest to him than the law. In 1794 he moved to Dresden, where he began to study the literature and culture of antiquity with incredible zeal. Dresden was the natural place to undertake this venture for it had one of the best collections of plaster casts of antiquities north of the Alps. In fact, it had been in Dresden that Winckelmann—who was very much an inspiration for Schlegel—began to lay the groundwork for his study of Greek art. What Winckelmann accomplished in the study of the plastic arts of antiquity, Schlegel hoped to accomplish in the study of literature of antiquity. In the years 1794–1795—at the advanced age of twenty-two and twenty-three—he wrote numerous essays on Greek literature. Among these is the essay *On the Study of Greek Poetry,* which was intended to serve as the introduction to a larger study entitled *The Greeks and Romans.* The study, however, was never completed. Schlegel sent *On the Study of Greek Poetry* to his publisher in 1795, where it languished for some time and was finally published two years later in 1797. By an unfortunate coincidence, Schiller's *On Naive and Sentimental Poetry*—which addresses many of the same issues as Schlegel's study—was published shortly before his own study appeared. Schlegel took care later to point out that he had no knowledge of this work during the composition of his essay. Indeed, he notes that if he had had knowledge of it, he might have been able to spare himself several infelicities.[2]

It is within this context, then, that the Romantic Schlegel took shape. A year after the publication of *On the Study of Greek Poetry,* Schlegel moved to Jena, where he made several important friendships, including those with Tieck and Schleiermacher. By the time the essay was actually published, Schlegel was concerning himself more and more with modern literature, with what he termed "Romantic" literature. Indeed, a year after its publication, Schlegel was publishing the *Athenäum,* the signal document and organ of the early Romantic movement. It was during this time—and by means of the *Athenäum*—that much of what came to define the Romantic sensibility was mapped out. Virtually all of the texts for which Schlegel is justly famous appeared in the *Athenäum*—a journal that lasted only two years.

At first glance, this period of transition would seem to constitute a remarkable about-face. Indeed, values, orientations, and goals would appear to be completely altered. Schlegel is usually characterized as a thinker of absolute self-reflexivity. Romanticism in turn is characterized as a completely new and radically distinct brand of literature. Schlegel's earlier work seems so markedly different from the common understanding of Schlegel that it is often simply ignored. Given the general impulse to present Schlegel as the embodiment and representative of Romanticism, the very question of a classicist Schlegel is a critical complication that many would prefer to avoid.[3] One must also consider the effect of the range of texts available in English by Schlegel. Despite the staggering array of studies Schlegel authored—the *Critical Friedrich Schlegel Edition* [*Kritische Friedrich Schlegel Ausgabe*] runs to thirty-five volumes—only two slim volumes of Schlegel's work are available in English. The contents of these volumes are drawn exclusively from Schlegel's Romanticist phase. As a result, a rather distorted and somewhat simplified understanding of both Schlegel and Romanticism has been made possible.[4] Nonetheless, the relation between the classical and Romantic writings constitutes a dimension to Schlegel's oeuvre that must be born in mind.[5] Not only must the existence of these "classicist" writings be acknowledged, but their relation to early Romanticism must also be studied.[6]

As a preliminary observation, it should be noted that even a superficial perusal of Schlegel's work suggests that a strictly "Romantic" assessment of Schlegel misses the mark. A remarkable number of the writings of the *Athenäum* period, for instance, deal directly with classical antiquity—and not in disparaging terms either.[7] For instance, Schlegel notes in one of the *Ideas*: "All the classical poems of the ancients are coherent, inseparable; they form an organic whole, they constitute, properly viewed, only a single poem, the only one in which poetry itself appears in perfection" (p. 102). Statements such as these are no doubt glossed over in the rush to make Schlegel conform to a preexistant understanding of Romanticism. Yet they are by no means anomalous and are evidence of not only an often neglected dimension but also a surprising continuity in Schlegel's work. Indeed, throughout the writings of the Romantic period, classical antiquity remains a persistent point of reference. Nor does this interest stop here. In the lectures on the history of European literature of 1803–1804, Schlegel devoted more than half of his time to considering Greek and Roman literature.[8] And in the *History of Ancient and Modern Literature* of 1812, the literature of antiquity still holds a prominent place. As Schlegel notes there: "Our intellectual development is so utterly based in that of the ancients that it is indeed incredibly difficult to discuss literature without beginning at this point."[9] It is not simply that Schlegel never lost his love of ancient literature. Rather, antiquity remained an integral part of Schlegel's understanding of literature. Moreover, antiquity was not something to be transcended and cast aside. Antiquity continued to define the parameters and standards according to which the achievement of modern literature was to be measured. In fact, modern literature was only truly modern in as much as it stood in relation to antiquity.[10]

The question of the relation of modernity to antiquity, of course, did not originate with Schlegel.[11] The so-called *querelle des anciens et des modernes* had been a focal point of critical concern for some time in Europe. It first took shape in the seventeenth century in the efforts of Descartes and Bacon and their followers to outline and defend a new experimental science. In order to do so, it was necessary to challenge and dispute the enormous authority of Aristotle. This quickly assumed the form of a debate on the relative superiority of the ancients versus the moderns. The essence of this debate was soon transferred to the literary realm, where it was bruted that the ancients could no longer serve as absolute standards of artistic production. For instance, Charles Perrault—whose reading of *The Century of Louis XIV* [*Le siècle de Louis le Grand*] in 1687 before the French academy is considered one of the major skirmishes in the *querelle*—argued that the ancient writers were full of errors that later ages had rendered obvious.[12] Fontenelle argued that not only were the ancients essentially no different than the moderns, and hence not unsurpassable, but that they suffered from the lack of accumulated wisdom and knowledge that the moderns possess. Despite such attacks, the ancients had a formidable defender in Nicolas Boileau-Despréaux, who emphasized the constant exemplary role the ancients played for various cultures throughout history.

A similar debate took place in England, beginning with writers such as Sir William Temple and William Wotton, who debated the ability of the moderns to improve upon the ancients. The debate reached its literary apogee in Swift's *An Account of the Battle between the Antient and Modern Books in St. James's Library* (1704), in which the books of the two camps literally do battle. Swift also addressed the topic in his *A Tale of the Tub* (1704), which ridiculed the pedantic pretentions of modern critics. More temperate writers such as Pope attempted to reconcile the two poles of the debate by suggesting in *An Essay in Criticism* that, as the ancients were exemplary imitators of nature, to imitate them would be to be faithful to nature.

The notion that antiquity provided the prototype for contemporary literary production became an increasingly vexed issue. With the collapse of mythology and the gradual erosion of Christianity's ability to substitute for a mythology, it became clear that the gap between antiquity and modernity was unbridgeable. Indeed, the insistence on the adherence to a classical background and context seemed to propel literature unavoidably toward the mock-heroic and satiric. To many this seemed the most straightforward way to acknowledge the incommensurability between these two cultural domains. Even Swift, in his defense of the ancients, assumed the mock heroic form. Thus, far from establishing the superiority of either, the debates in France and England confirmed the thoroughgoing distinctiveness of ancient and modern culture.

In Germany the *querelle* took a slightly different turn. Undergirding the debate in England and France were certain assumptions about the ease of accessibility and translatability that obtained between modernity and antiquity. In Germany, however, antiquity and modernity came to be seen as irrevocably distinct from one another. The work of Herder did much to facilitate this development as he emphasized that a radical cultural relativism was at work throughout history. As each culture was unique and operated according to its own specific rules, it was pointless to turn to another culture for models to be imitated. What was to be imitated was the inimitable. This position ironically secured the status of the ancients to a considerable extent, for the ancients were inimitable. Thus, for instance, Homer can figure as an Ossian-like writer worthy of adulation in Goethe's *The Sorrows of Young Werther*. Winckelmann likewise served to strengthen the position of the ancients as a paradoxically inimitable model. Hence the ancients were secured in their status to such an extent that it seemed to amount to—as E. M. Butler memorably phrased it—the tyranny of Greece over Germany. The *querelle* in Germany culminated in Schiller's *On Naive and Sentimental Poetry* (1795–1976). Yet, while Schiller accorded exemplarity to the ancients, his discussion was predicated upon the thoroughgoing distinctness of antiquity and modernity. Modernity was conditioned by an utterly unique set of circumstances; it could not simply imitate nature because it had entered the philosophically inaugurated era of self-reflexivity. Moreover, these traits are not to be wished away; they comprise the very task of modernity—to account for the self-reflexivity of consciousness. While Schiller did much to justify a post-Kantian aesthetic theory vis-à-vis the ancients, he did not draw out the radical implications it contained for the understanding of modernity. Schiller could not resolve the antinomy between antiquity and modernity. It was Schlegel who assessed this large-scale historical dilemma and drew from it radical conclusions about literary and cultural production.[13]

This search for a modern culture, however, should not blind us to the fact that no theory emerges *de novo*. Modernity could only be conceptualized within the vocabulary of antiquity; it could only be articulated *in relation to* antiquity. Even writings that seem to focus exclusively on antiquity or modernity often have the relation between the two—and thus both antiquity and modernity—as their founding premise. This relation must be born in mind when considering Schlegel's early work. It is indeed tempting to assume that, because he relentlessly focused on the literature of antiquity in his early writings, modernity is simply not a matter of concern. If modernity is alluded to it is usually in the most disparaging and dismissive of tones.[14] According to this logic, then, Schlegel sided entirely with the ancients in this debate and then for some reason made a complete about-face, rejected antiquity, and embraced modernity.[15] If this assessment were accurate, it would certainly relegate the early writings to the status of muddled juvenalia. It would also tend to simplify Romanticism itself. Yet any careful consideration of these early writings of Schlegel must come to the conclusion that they derive their full meaning from this larger debate about modernity—to which Romanticism itself was one response.[16] As Richard Brinkmann notes of *On the Study of Greek Poetry:* "From the outset this text is very decidedly concerned with modern literature and nothing else right up until the end."[17] This subtextual and contextual perspective must be taken into account in any consideration of Schlegel's writings from his "classicist" phase.[18]

It is this large-scale, historical perspective that characterizes Schlegel's approach to questions of literature from his "classicist" phase to his Romantic phase and on through his so-called Catholic-Conservative phase.[19] It would be easy to conclude from much of the secondary literature in English that Schlegel, when he was not thinking obsessively about irony, only considered literature in a vacuum. Yet, despite what some critics have implied, Schlegel did not think of literature in purely abstract terms. As Schlegel commented to his brother, August Wilhem, he found any theory not founded in history to be ridiculous.[20] Schlegel's conception of literature was, from beginning to end, profoundly historical. Whatever pronouncements Schlegel did make about literature as such were always based upon detailed and rigorous historical study.[21] Hence it is not just that the literature of antiquity consistently played a role in Schlegel's thought. Rather, it is that Schlegel's notion of Romanticism was from the outset predicated upon a broad, historical study of literature. Romanticism, accordingly, was not seen simply as a moment within which literature became conscious of itself; it was also seen as the fruition of the history of Western literature itself. Indeed, the very impetus for the conceptualization of the Romantic—which *On the Study of Greek Poetry* articulates—was the search for a resolution to a cultural dilemma of massive historical proportions between classical and postclassical literature. It is tempting to think of Romanticism as a complete departure from the past, as a "new class of poetry," as Wordsworth termed it in the preface to *Lyrical Ballads.* Yet one should recall that, for many artists (such as Hölderlin, Goethe, Schiller, Kleist, Shelley, and Keats among others), antiquity often provided the medium within which to articulate a literature that would be truly modern.[22] Thus Romanticism— precisely because of its ambition to define modernity—is predicated on an exegetical reading of the past. *On the Study of Greek Poetry* was part of this larger struggle to recast classical literature to such a radical extent that modernity would thereby be made possible.

As many have noted, *On the Study of Greek Poetry* is an essay at odds with itself. The essay seeks to defend antiquity at the same time that it seeks to offer a corrective to the development of contemporary literature. It argues that the crisis of modernity begins already with the collapse of classical culture. With the disintegration of the Roman Empire and the abandonment of Latin as a lingua franca, European culture began to fragment into more and more particular and idiosyncratic forms. While it initially seemed that Christianity might be able to provide a unifying medium, eventually particularity won out. Before the implications of the historical contours of the essay can be teased out, it is necessary to clarify what may appear to be some of the conceptual idiosyncrasies intrinsic to this essay. Romanticism, for instance, here designates not a literary movement that came to prominence at the end of the eighteenth century; rather, it designates a large historical period—essentially, postantiquity. In this sense, the term derives from the conceptual link to the breakdown of Latin into various vernacular languages, that is, the Romance languages.[23]

The difficulty inherent in the relation between classical and postclassical culture according to Schlegel is that it is not characterized by a break or rupture in development. Rather, both antiquity and modernity are governed by two distinct and incommensurable principles of development (or *Bildung*).[24] What Schlegel presents is the conflict between two different types of *Bildung*. Antiquity is governed by a natural *Bildung*. It is characterized by a consistent fidelity to nature itself. This fidelity, however, is tempered by a commitment to the characteristic as opposed to the idiosyncratic. In the process of its development, natural *Bildung* is oriented therefore to what is essential to nature. The culture that thereby results is as authentic and true to nature as it is possible for culture to be. Indeed, it may bring to presence what is only implicit within nature itself. While natural *Bildung* does achieve a perfection, it follows an organicist logic that dictates that such perfection can only be fleeting. A natural decay and decline necessarily follow perfection. Accordingly, antiquity is a closed and completed cycle, an evolutionary process come to full fruition.

Modernity is characterized by an artificial *Bildung*, which is led by concepts and not nature. To a great extent, modernity has been dominated by a sterile neoclassicism that attempted to dictate terms to culture on the basis of an inaccurately interpreted antiquity. When modernity does turn to consider nature, it focuses on the individual and idiosyncratic and thus deviates more and more from nature. As a result, much of modern culture is anarchic, incapable of establishing a modern form of art that could become the basis for a broad-based culture in general. Despite these apparent limitations, however, modernity is capable of endless progress. Thus Schlegel remains optimistic in the essay that this is just a passing crisis even though he himself concedes that it is an apparently hopeless imbroglio.[25] Indeed, Schlegel pins great hopes on a coming aesthetic revolution that will transform modern culture.[26]

Interestingly, one of the main factors in this revolution is criticism. Criticism is one of the defining features of modern culture and it does not necessarily have to produce false concepts to guide artistic production—as it does in neoclassicism. In fact, criticism could produce correct concepts for artistic production. Criticism then offers itself as a third term, a point of possible synthesis. This possibility is not fully explored in this essay, but the foundation for a solution to the dilemma between antiquity and modernity is outlined. Criticism thus is a possible way to resolve the deadlock between antiquity and modernity; it also proposes the way to establish an aesthetically valid culture. Criticism, moreover, should not be the distilled abstraction of this dilemma. Rather, criticism should be the historically informed comprehension of this dilemma. The difficulty within the essay is that the solution is sought for within one of the constituent elements of the debate. Whereas the only solution is to be found within the process of the study and critique of the issues.

As Kant lays much of the foundation for Schlegel's thought, it is worthwhile to consider briefly his aesthetics.[27] In the *Critique of Judgment* Kant argued that the judgment involved in the assessment of beauty was of a distinct order. Although it took the form of a judgment, it did not lead to knowledge. Unlike epistemologically motivated judgments, which proceed by means of determinative judgment, that is, the application of an existing concept to a particular instance, aesthetic judgments proceed by means of reflective judgment. Reflective judgment begins with a particular instance—an instance of beauty—and searches for an appropriate concept, which it does not find. As a result, the imagination—which usually renders an image to which the understanding can apply a concept—is put into a state of free play. In this state of free play the mind is made aware of the constitutive role it plays in the production of knowledge. More important, because this judgment is based on disinterested pleasure, it allows mind to become aware of itself as a subjective universality. That is, mind becomes aware of the universal aspect of mind. It is this dimension of aesthetic judgment that allows it to become the bridge between epistemology and ethics. Aesthetic judgment is the propadeutic for the universalist thinking necessary for ethical action. This is because, for Kant, ethical action is dependent upon the reflection as to whether a particular action would make the basis for a valid, universal law for all of humanity. Aesthetic judgment thus assumes the form and structure of ethics. While many aspects of Kant's aesthetics were recast, the notion of the aesthetic being the philosophical bridge to ethics was widely taken up by many writers. Indeed, even twentieth-century critics, who inaccurately accused Kant of being the progenitor of a formalist and apolitical aesthetics, accepted this notion without reservation.

Kant's notion of aesthetics rested upon the Enlightenment assumption of a universal reason. Two distinct reinterpretations were made of this assumption during the eighteenth century. The first emerged out of the counter-Enlightenment current prevalent in many of the German-speaking parts of Europe, which introduced the notion of the nonuniversal character of reason.

That is, reason was characterized as being fragmented into distinct historical periods and cultures. Accordingly, reason was not universal but contingent and relative. Once these notions were incorporated into a historically informed aesthetic theory, contemplating Greek culture became a more complicated affair. It no longer seemed that the Greeks established a cultural standard that could simply be replicated by another culture. Thus, even though the Greeks remained a cultural ideal, they essentially became a frustratingly unattainable ideal. The problem then became how to redirect modern culture using Greek culture as a point of orientation. This accounts for the supposition of two incommensurable cultural realms present in many treatises on aesthetics at this time. Schiller's *On Naive and Sentimental Poetry* and Schlegel's *On the Study of Greek Poetry* are perhaps the most well-known instances of this predicament. This explains the perhaps confusing presence of an almost neoclassical yearning for antiquity together with the firm conviction that contemporary culture is irrevocably distinct from antiquity.

The second reinterpretation emerged out of the transformation of Kant's philosophy at the hands of such thinkers as Fichte and Schelling. It soon came to be seen as intolerable that Kant had banished elements that normally were an integral part of philosophy to the realm of the unknowable. Two elements in particular—God and the world—were reduced by Kant to mere regulative ideas. They were forever closed off from philosophy and served merely a heuristic function. An effort was thus undertaken to reintegrate these elements into philosophy. Fichte found a compromise that granted reality to the world but made it merely the externalization of a transcendental ego. Soon this seemed to grant only an intangible reality to the natural world. Schelling responded with a philosophy of nature that granted much more autonomy to the natural world. These reformulations within German Idealism were to have an impact on the aesthetic theories of the time. Indeed, as Schelling suggested in the final chapter of his *System of Transcendental Idealism,* art constituted not simply an element but the full realization of idealism. This is because art comes closest to the world-producing activity of the Absolute.[28]

Schlegel for his part historicizes Kantian aesthetic theory by means of antiquity.[29] For Kant, disinterested pleasure was to allow apprehension of the formal purposeless purposiveness of a work of art. This state—which is essentially transhistorical in nature—permits the free play that the suspension of determinative judgment allows. Schlegel projects this state into antiquity, where a disinterested pleasure supposedly ruled. Such a move allows Schlegel to historicize what is otherwise just a subjective state. It also allows Schlegel to render this Kantian aesthetic ideal unattainable because it has been situated within an irrecoverable past. For Schlegel it is not a matter of reinstating a transhistorical aesthetic disposition. The only way to this state is by means of the *study* of antiquity. For the study of antiquity—the study of that phase of culture in which culture was characterized by disinterested pleasure—provides the historical content for aesthetic contemplation. Thus not only is Kantian aesthetics historicized but the Fichtean notion of the formal reflexivity of the transcendental subject is given a concrete ground in something truly beyond it. What Schlegel adds here is that self-reflexivity is a difficult venture in that the transcendental subject does not externalize itself in a not-I that can be dispensed with once its provenance is realized. The externalized other to the transcendental subject remains resistant because it forms a complex historical web that does not yield to a purely formal analysis.[30]

Modernity also has an impact on this historico-philosophical vision of literature. For modernity becomes characterized by the subject's awareness of its fall from a harmonious—albeit deluded—conjunction with an objective world. Modernity is thus the endless self-reflection upon the unattainable.[31] Much like Schelling, Schlegel was clearly dissatisfied with the notion of nature, the empirical, being simply the empty negation of the subject that has been posited by the subject itself so that it might come to know its own transcendental activity. Schlegel did not conceive of the empirical as an objective externalization of a transcendental subjectivity. Rather, in Schlegel's thought the empirical acquires its own relative autonomy; it acquires a distinct history. In fact, as Ernst Behler has persuasively argued, Schlegel anticipates Hegel's resolutions to the dilemmas of Fichtean idealism. Like Hegel, Schlegel injects a profoundly historical dimension into German Idealism.[32] If a transcendental subject has externalized itself into the empirical, resolution cannot be accomplished by means of a contentless, formalistic analysis such as Fichte's.[33] Instead, it is the content, nature, and evolution of the empirical that must be accounted for. It is precisely by means of a philosophy that embraces and accounts for the empirical that the consciousness of the empirical comes into being, or, rather, that an objectified subjectivity reclaims its status as subjectivity. Culture, accordingly, acquires a historico-philosophical dimension; it is the temporally contoured intersubjective expression and manifestation of subjectivity in general.[34] Yet the culture of antiquity—by being so historically distant—has assumed the status of nature. Despite being the product of subjectivity, it stands opposed to subjectivity as something distant, external, and objective.[35] This is why too much emphasis cannot be made on the "study" in *On the Study of Greek Poetry*.[36] For this essay truly turns on the notion of the *study* of antiquity. It is the study of antiquity—which is only possible in modernity—that truly brings antiquity to completion.[37]

While *On the Study of Greek Poetry* may seem to be a conflicted and self-contradictory essay—which in fact it is—it is so for compelling and logical reasons. Schlegel attempts to think through to the necessarily contradictory conclusion the contemporary understanding of antiquity and modernity.[38] Schlegel's treatment of antiquity does indeed take part in the cultural nostalgia of the time. Yet, in Schlegel's case, this nostalgia is tempered by a historical and theoretical perspicacity. It is this awareness that leads to the realization that antiquity cannot be re-created. Schlegel consistently argues against a neoclassicism as it was practiced in the seventeenth and eighteenth centuries. Instead, Schlegel attempts to reconceptualize modernity via antiquity. Modernity is predicated upon a revaluation of antiquity. This is an important perspective to bear in mind for the relation to antiquity in the essay can easily be confusing. Any text so strongly in favor of the culture of antiquity and so despairing of the culture of modernity would seem to be culturally reactionary. At the same time, however, the essay laments the destructive influence of the culture of antiquity on modernity and retains hope for a culture yet to come. According to the essay, modernity is predicated upon a reinterpretation, a redescription of antiquity. A valid modernity requires the reassessment of the past. Indeed, the future can only come to be if the past was altered.

This revaluation was made possible by the ongoing work of reception as well as continuing archaeological discoveries. The discovery of Herculaneum, for instance, stimulated a renewed interest in the art of antiquity in the eighteenth century.[39] Most important, however, antiquity began to be examined with a greater attention to historical and artifactual detail. This necessitated the conceptualization of Greek art as a distinct entity within antiquity. To discuss Greek art in terms more appropriate for the culture of antiquity as a whole was increasingly seen to falsify Greek art. As Ernst Behler points out:

> This revaluation also brought about a decisive change in the prevalent relationship to classical antiquity, which can be described as a departure from the dominant Roman and Aristotelian influence upon European criticism in exchange for a closer bond with the Greeks and especially with the Platonic tradition. Previously, the Greeks had maintained their impact on the history of aesthetics chiefly through the Romans as well as through various adaptations of Aristotle's *Poetics*. Following Winckelmann and the tradition of German humanism, the Schlegels attempted to terminate this form of classicism by establishing a close connection with the aesthetic world of the Greeks and by referring directly to pronouncements on poetry by Plato and the Greek rhetoricians.[40]

Behler's observations go a long way to explain the often confusing alternating praise and condemnation of both antiquity and modernity in Schlegel's essay. Terms are not being confused; rather, they are being differentiated beyond their traditional definitions.

As Behler notes, inspiring Schlegel in this avenue of thought was the work of Winckelmann. While it is impossible to do Winckelmann justice in the context of these introductory remarks, it is necessary to consider briefly his significance in light of Schlegel's early work. For, as Schlegel himself claimed, he wanted to be the Winckelmann of Greek poetry. Not only did Winckelmann help to establish standards in the study of art history, but he helped to define the specific interest in Greek art in the eighteenth century.[41] He worked to isolate an antiquity proper from later Hellenistic and Roman imitations. Accordingly, it was this later and debased form of antiquity that was the basis for the sterile neoclassicism of the eighteenth century. Winckelmann thus opened the way for a seemingly contradictory anti-neo-classicist classicism. Yet Winckelmann's aim was not simply to awaken an appreciation of Greek art. Rather, Winckelmann was presenting an aesthetic theory as well. He forged a path out of the strictures of the baroque and rococo styles, the neoclassical style, and the incipient realism of the modern style. The question at stake in all of these styles concerns the issue of imitation. What exactly is to be imitated? Should it be the exempla of artistic style to be found in Greek art? Or should one imitate nature itself directly? It is in these terms, after all, that the *querelle* articulated itself. Winckelmann considered this a false dichotomy. What the Greeks offered were not works of art to be slavishly imitated; rather, the Greeks offered works that were evidence of a certain artistic methodology. For what the Greeks did was to study nature, distilling from it a beauty that nature itself could only articulate in a piecemeal fashion. Thus an ideal was to be abstracted from the real. It is not imitation in any real sense of the term. What one learns from the Greeks is the process of an idealizing imitation—or potentiation—of nature. Yet this is a process of idealization that is not a work of fantasy but a realization of what is yet to be expressed by nature.

Winckelmann also articulated a historically informed view of art that saw a time period as possessing a structural evolution that manifested itself throughout all the art works of a specific field. Winckelmann thereby endowed the study of culture with a much richer dimensionality. It was not merely that the Greeks were a distinct and autonomous culture, but that Greek culture had a coherent and integral history that unfolded itself through the developmental stages of various artistic forms. Winckelmann's work had great implications for the study of literature, as Schlegel quickly realized. On the one hand, it called for a far more rigorous examination of individual works. On the other hand, it also called for a careful study of the entire cultural context within which a work finds itself. This is precisely the perspective Schlegel draws in to the study of literature. Schlegel sought to join together a critical interpretation of individual works with a historical understanding of literature in general.

All these elements came together to form a historico-philosophical literary theory. Indeed, one could term it a philosophy that was articulating itself by means of literary criticism. If the Absolute does externalize itself into the empirical, then it was not adequate to view this externalization as an essentially repetitive and atemporal act. There was a logic and a reason to this externalization. It was necessary to examine this articulation of the Absolute as a historical process. Thus the study of Greek culture as a coherent whole is part of the study of the Absolute itself. Moreover, the study itself becomes thereby part of the articulation of the Absolute. The historical understanding of the past becomes part of the historical unfolding of the Absolute. This is a crucial aspect of Schlegel's work, the importance of which it is impossible to overestimate. It is the conscious apprehension of the past articulations of the Absolute that comprises the full articulation of the Absolute. It is in the consciousness—that is, the philosophy—of past material externalizations of the Absolute that the gap between the Absolute and finitude begins to be bridged. Thus the title, *On the Study of Greek Poetry*, is at once precise and deceptive.

A cursory reading of Schlegel's essay could easily conclude that all of modern culture is to be abandoned in favor of a culture modeled on that of antiquity's. A good deal of attention is devoted to modernity in *On the Study of Greek Poetry*. It is often decried and shown in poor comparison with antiquity. Accordingly, modern literature seems to be catering increasingly to a jaded sensibility that requires ever more violent stimulants. To conclude, however, that this is the sum total of this essay's view of modernity does not do justice to the complexities of Schlegel's historico-philosophical vision. For not only does Schlegel disclose that the simple imitation of antiquity is pointless, but he clearly indicates that modern culture might be on the brink of a sudden transformation. Moreover, there are harbingers of what such a transformed culture might look like. Shakespeare, for instance, provides an indication of the possible vitality of modern culture.[42] The essential task of modernity, therefore, is to diagnose and move beyond both antiquity and what has up until then defined modernity. Indeed, as Schlegel commented to his brother August in 1794, the fundamental task of modernity is to synthesize what is essentially classical and modern.

For the most part, however, *On the Study of Greek Poetry* does not successfully outline how a synthesis between antiquity and modernity might be achieved. It remains very much caught up in outlining the thesis and antithesis that antiquity and modernity present. Indeed, the antinomy between the two seems irreconcilable in the essay. It is not difficult to see Romanticism—as Schlegel was later to conceive it—as this synthesis.[43] In this sense Romanticism is to be seen as founded on the diagnosis and analysis of antiquity and modernity.[44] As such, it is not founded—as it is often assumed to be—upon an empty and formal self-reflexivity but upon a critical history. Schlegel thereby expands and complicates the ambitions of post-Kantian thinkers to reconcile the Kantian *Ding-an-sich* with a transcendental subject by insisting upon the reinscription of the products of mind.[45]

Romanticism, as literature's own production of a theory of itself, provides a resolution to the theoretical dilemma Schlegel outlines in *On the Study of Greek Poetry*. As Schlegel acknowledges in this essay, there is no real possibility of returning to a precritical state. There can be no direct and immediate relation to the world once the notion of phenomenality has taken root.[46] The only real relation possible is a mediate one, one that achieves awareness of the medium of its access. While the Kantian subject suffers an apparently permanent separation from the world, an isotropic affinity is created in post-Kantian thought between the mediated relation between the subject and world and the endless self-mediation of a transcendental subject and the material world. For Schlegel, this isotropic affinity is evidenced most clearly in the work of art. For the work of art—by means of criticism—reveals a structural relation to the infinitude of such transcendental activity. As Walter Benjamin phrases it: "Criticism is thus the medium in which the limitedness of the individual work relates itself methodically to the endlessness of art and into which it is ultimately transposed, for art—as it itself understands itself—is a medium of endless reflection."[47] The completion, the true realization of antiquity can only happen in modernity—more precisely, in the literary theory and literary history that is possible in modernity.[48] Accordingly, Romanticism itself—as a literally literary theory—is the realization of antiquity.

On the Study of Greek Poetry raises more issues and problems than it can possibly solve. It is a process of struggle, a conceptual Laocöon statuary. As Peter Szondi has suggested, the essay is the document not so much of a standpoint as of an evolution.[49] For this reason, it may seem to contradict not only the later Schlegel but its own argument as well. Nonetheless, the essay remains an incisive and penetrating examination of issues central to the aesthetic and philosophical debates at the turn of the nineteenth century. What the patient reader is rewarded with is a deeper understanding of the effort to define and elaborate a modern culture in the eighteenth century. The historical dimension is doubly important here in that one gains in the course of the essay a broader appreciation of the historical origins of Romanticism in addition to an appreciation of the importance of history for Romanticism. Indeed, what Schlegel presents here in crucible form is an etiology of the profound cultural transformation that was taking place at the end of the eighteenth century and that would culminate in Romanticism. It is, as Ernst Behler has justly suggested, the "Oldest System Program of Romanticism."[50]

On the Study of Greek Poetry

ON THE STUDY OF GREEK POETRY

It is obvious that *modern poetry*[1] either *has not yet attained the goal*
towards which it is striving, or that its striving has no established goal, its
development [*Bildung*][2] no specific direction, the sum of its history no regular
continuity, the whole no unity.[3] Granted, it is not lacking in works in whose
inexhaustible contents the inquisitive admiration loses itself, and from whose
towering heights the astonished eye averts itself. Nor is it lacking in works
whose overpowering might sweeps up and conquers all hearts. Yet the strongest
shock, the most boundless activity, is often the least *satisfying.* Even the most
splendid poems of the moderns—the great vigor and art of which demand
reverence—frequently unify the mind only to rend it in an even more painful
fashion. They leave a thorn in the soul and take more than they give.[4] *Satisfac-*
tion occurs only in complete pleasure, where every excited expectation is
fulfilled and even the smallest disquietude is resolved—where all longing
ceases. This is what is missing from the poetry of our age! Not an abundance of
individual,[5] splendid beauties, but *harmony* and *completion* and the quiet and
satisfaction that can only come from these; a *complete beauty* that would be
whole and *persevering;* a Juno that would not become a cloud in the moment of
the most fiery embrace.[6] Thus art is not undone because of all those who—
being not coarse so much as wrongheaded and more miseducated [*mißgebildet*]
than uneducated [*ungebildet*]—willingly allow their imaginations to be filled
with everything that is unusual or new only in order to fill the infinite emptiness of their minds with something so that they might escape the intolerable
expanse of their existence for a few moments. The name of art is profaned if by
poetry one understands toying with fantastic or childish images in order to
stimulate indolent desires, to titillate dull senses, and to cater to coarse pleasures. Yet everywhere where genuine culture [*Bildung*] has not reached all the
people, there will be a *vulgar* art that knows only the allure of base voluptuous-
ness and loathsome intensity. Despite the constant alternation of its content, its
spirit remains always the same: muddled exiguity. Nonetheless, there is also a
better class of art, whose works stand out from the more common works like
high cliffs out of the vague fog bank of a distant region. Every now and then in
the recent history of art we come across poets who, in the midst of an oblivious

age, appear to be foreigners from a nobler world. With all the strength their minds can marshal, they seek the *eternal*. If they do not entirely achieve harmony and satisfaction in their works, they nonetheless strive so ardently for precisely this that they raise the most justified hope that the goal of poetry will not remain forever unattainable if it can be attained by other means, such as namely force and art, culture [*Bildung*] and science. It is solely in this better class of art that the shortcomings of modern poetry are most clearly revealed. Precisely here—when sensibility has recognized the great worth of a poem, and judgment has tested and confirmed the verdicts of sensibility—the understanding ends up in a considerable embarrassment. In most cases, it appears that that about which art should be most proud does not even belong to it. It is a true merit of modern poetry that so much that was good and noble—and that was misunderstood, suppressed, and banished from the general mindset, from society, and from the wisdom of the schools—received from it at times protection and shelter, and at other times succor and a home. Here, essentially in the one unsullied place in an unholy century, the few who were noble laid the fruits of their exalted existence—the best of all that they did, thought, enjoyed, and strove for—on the altar of humanity. Yet is not truth and morality—rather than beauty—more often than not the aim of these poets? Just analyze the intention of the artist, regardless whether he clearly reveals them or whether he follows his instincts without any clear consciousness; analyze the judgments of the experts and the decisions of the public! Almost

[219] everywhere you will find just about every other principle silently presupposed or implicitly put forth as the highest goal and fundamental law of art, as the ultimate measure for the worth of their works. Every principle, that is, except that of *beauty*. This is to such an extent not the governing principle of modern poetry that many of its most splendid works are openly representations of the *ugly*. One must finally, if reluctantly, admit that there does indeed exist a representation of confusion in all its plenitude, of despair characterized by boundless vigor, that demands an equal if not greater creative power and artistic wisdom than is required for the representation of abundance and vigor

[89M] in complete harmony. The most praised modern poems appear to be different from this type [of art] more in degree than manner. If a faint hint of perfect beauty is found, it is experienced not so much in serene enjoyment as in *unsatisfied longing*. The more vigorously one strives after it, the more one distances oneself from the beautiful. The *boundaries* of science and art, of the true and the beautiful, are so confused that even the conviction that those eternal boundaries are permanent has generally begun to falter for the most part. Philosophy poeticizes and poetry philosophizes:[7] history is treated as poetry and poetry is treated as history. Even the types of poetry exchange their very definition. A lyrical mood becomes the object of a drama, and dramatic material is forced into lyrical form. This *anarchy* is not confined to the outer limits; rather, it spans the entire realm of taste and art. The creative force is restless and fickle; the individual as well as public receptivity is always as insatiable and it is unsatisfied. Theory itself appears to despair utterly of a *fixed point* in the endless flux. Public taste—yet how could a public taste be possible where there are no public morals?—or, rather, the caricature of public taste, *fashion,* pays homage with every passing moment to a new false idol. Each new splendid appearance inspires the confident belief that now the goal—ultimate beauty—has been attained and that, accordingly, the fundamental law of taste, [220] the ultimate measure of all works of art has been found. All so that the next moment can put an end to the giddiness, so that those who have come to their senses can destroy the image of the mortal idol, and in a new affected intoxication enshrine another in its place whose divinity will not last longer than the mood of its worshipers! Some artists strive for the sumptuous charms of a voluptuous material, the resplendent ornamentation, the caressing melody of an enchanting language, even if their fantastic writing affronts truth and propriety and leaves the soul empty. Some artists delude themselves because of a certain polish and refinement in organization and execution with the premature and erroneous impression of perfection. While others, unconcerned with charm and polish, consider a touching fidelity in representation and the most profound understanding of the most obscure peculiarity[8] as the highest goal of art. This one-sided taste of the Italians, French, and English is to be found reunited in all its harsh severity in Germany. The metaphysical investigations of a few thinkers into the nature of the beautiful did not have the slightest influence on the development [*Bildung*] of taste and art. However, the practical theory of poetry was, other than a few exceptions, until now not much more than the *sense* of that which one already did incorrectly enough—as if it were [90M] the distilled concept of false taste, the spirit of an infelicitous history. Poetic theory follows naturally enough those three main directions, and seeks for the goal of art one moment in *charm,* the next moment in *correctness,* and then the next in *truth.* With the stamp of its authority it sometimes recommended sanctioned works as eternal *models of imitation;*[9] at other times it presented *absolute originality* as the greatest measure of all works of art, and covered the [221] slightest hint of imitation with infinite ignominy. It strictly demands, in scholastic armature, unconditional submission, even to its most arbitrary and obviously foolish laws. Or it deifies genius in mystical oracles, makes artistic anarchy the fundamental principle, and honors manifestations that were often very dubious with impressive myths. The hope—to invent living works by means of theorems, to construct beautiful plays according to concepts—has been disappointed so often that, in the place of belief, an extreme indifference has finally settled in. Theory has only itself to thank that it has lost all credence with artists

of genius as well as the public! How can it demand reverence for its pronouncements and obedience for its laws when it has not even succeeded in rendering a
proper explanation of the nature of the poetic arts and a satisfactory classification of its types? When it has come to no agreement about the determination of
art in general? If there is one claim to which all the adherents of the various
aesthetic systems appear to agree to a certain extent, it is that there is no
universally valid law of art, no constant goal of taste—or if there is such a
thing, it is not practical—and that the correctness of taste and the beauty of art
depend solely upon coincidence. And indeed *coincidence* alone appears to be at
work here; it appears to rule as an absolute despot in this strange realm of
confusion. The anarchy that is so noticeable in aesthetic theory as well as in the
praxis of artists spans the *history* of modern poetry. At first glance a common
element running through the whole barely allows itself to be discovered—to
say nothing of orderliness in its progression, specific stages in its development
[*Bildung*], distinct boundaries between its parts, and a satisfactory unity in the
whole.[10] In poet after poet one finds no enduring peculiarity. There is no

[222]   common background to be found in the spirit of contemporaneous works.
Among the moderns it is simply a devout wish that the spirit of a great master,
the spirit of a felicitous age, could widely disperse its beneficent effects, yet

[91M]   without the spirit that would be held in common thereby effacing the peculiarity of the individual, injuring its rights, or crippling its inventive power. An
endless swarm of the most wretched imitators follows every great original
artist—as long as he is born by the tide of fashion—until finally the originary
image has become so common and loathsome because of the eternal repetitions
and distortions that, in the place of deification, there enters abhorrence or
eternal oblivion. *Lack of character* seems to be the only characteristic of modern
poetry; *confusion* the common theme running throughout it; *lawlessness* the
spirit of its history; and *skepticism* the result of its theory. Even peculiarity does
not seem to have specific and fixed boundaries. French, English, Italian, and
Spanish poetry often seem to exchange their national characters, as if they were
in a masquerade. German poetry almost presents a complete geographical
specimen collection of all national characteristics of every age and every area of
the world: only the German, one notes, is missing. Utterly indifferent at
bottom to all form, and full only of an unquenchable thirst for *content,* the
more refined public demands of artists only *interesting individuality.* As long as
there is an *effect,* as long as the effect is *strong and new,* the public is as
indifferent to the manner in which—as well as the content within which—it
occurs as it is to the agreement of the individual effects to form a complete
whole. Art does what it can to satisfy this longing. Here one finds—as if one
were in a general store of aesthetics—folk poetry and courtly poetry next to
each other. Even the metaphysician can find there his own assortment. There

are Nordic or Christian epopees for the admirers of the north and Christianity; ghost stories for the lovers of mystical horrors, Iroquoian or cannibalistic odes [223] for the lovers of cannibalism; Greek costume[11] for antique souls; knightly poems for heroic tongues; and even national poetry for the dilettantes of Germanness! Nonetheless, it is pointless to draw out of all these realms the richest abundance of interesting individuality! The jar of the Danaïds remains eternally empty.[12] With every pleasure the desires become only more violent; with every allowance the demands rise ever higher, and the hopes for final satisfaction become ever more distant. The new becomes old; the unusual becomes common; the frisson of what is charming becomes dull. With its own power and artistic drive diminished, languid receptivity subsides into an appalling impotence. Taste thus weakened ultimately desires no other fare than repugnant crudities, until it finally dies off and becomes a distinct void. Even if [92M] vitality is not vanquished, however, little is gained. Like a man of noble mind who lacks, however, harmony—as the poet says of himself:

> I reel from desire to enjoyment
> And in enjoyment languish after desire[13]

—the vigorous aesthetic disposition strives and yearns restlessly in unsatisfied longing so that the agony of futile effort often culminates in a wretched despair.

When one considers with equal care the purposelessness and lawlessness of the whole of modern poetry as well as the true excellence of its individual parts then the sum of it appears like an ocean of warring forces, where the parts of the dissipated beauty, the fragments of shattered art, move confusedly [224] through one another in a lugubrious mixture. One could call it a *chaos* of everything sublime, beautiful, and charming, which—just like the Chaos of old out of which, according to legend, the world emerged—awaits a *love* and a *hatred* in order to separate the different parts and to unify the similar parts.

Is there no *guiding thread* to be found in order to solve this puzzling confusion, in order to find a way out of this labyrinth? The origin, interrelation, and ground of the many unusual idiosyncrasies of modern poetry must in some way be explicable. Perhaps it is possible for us to discover from the spirit of its previous history the *meaning* of its current efforts, the *direction* of its further course, and its future goal. If we could be certain of the *principle of its development* [*Bildung*] perhaps it would not be that difficult to unravel from this its *whole purpose*. Previously a pressing need often produced its object; out of despair emerged a new calm; and anarchy became the mother of a benevolent *revolution*.[14] Cannot the aesthetic anarchy of our age expect a similar *felicitous catastrophe*?[15] Perhaps the *decisive moment* has arrived—either taste will undergo a thorough improvement following which it can never regress but must necessarily move forward or art will always continue to decline and our age must surrender all hope for beauty and the reestablishment of a genuine art. Once we have comprehended more precisely the *character* of modern poetry, discovered the principle of its development [*Bildung*], and *explained* the most *original traits* of its individuality, the following questions will press themselves

[93M]   upon us:

> *What is the task of modern poetry?—*
> *Can it be attained?—*
> *What are the means to this?—*

[225]   It is clear that in the strictest and most literal sense there can be no characterlessness. What one tends to term an absence of character is either a character that has become very effaced and essentially unreadable or a character that is extremely complex, complicated, and puzzling. There is indeed a *common element* in that thorough anarchy evident throughout the entirety of modern poetry, a *characteristic trait* that could not exist if there were no *common inner foundation.* We are accustomed to considering modern poetry as a coherent whole more according to an obscure feeling than clearly articulated principles. But by what right do we tacitly presuppose this? It is true that, despite all the peculiarities and differences of the individual nations, the European peoples nonetheless betray—through the noticeably similar spirit that is apparent in the languages, the mindsets, customs, and institutions (as well as in many other traces that have remained of an earlier time)—the similar and common origin of their culture. In addition, there is a common religion that differs markedly from[16] all others. Beyond this, the culture [*Bildung*] of this extremely remarkable conglomeration of peoples is intimately intertwined, thoroughly interrelated; the individual parts constantly influence one another. It has, despite all differences, so many common characteristics, strives so obviously after one common goal, that it hardly can be considered as anything but a *whole.* What is true of the whole is true of the individual parts: like modern culture [*Bildung*] in general, modern poetry is an interrelated whole. As reasonable and as clear as this observation may be for many, there will certainly be no lack of those who will doubt—who will both deny this interrelation and explain it as being due to coincidental circumstances and not to a common principle. This is not the place to sort this out. It is enough that it is worth the effort to follow this lead and undertake the attempt to determine whether this general presupposition withstands examination. Already the *reciprocally influ-*

[226]   *encing* aspects of modern poetry point to an inner interrelation. Since the reestablishment of the sciences there has occurred among the different national poetries of the greatest and most cultivated European peoples a constant *re-*

ciprocal imitation. The Italian manner as well as French and English manner had their Golden Ages in which they despotically ruled over the taste of all the [94M] rest of cultivated Europe. Only Germany has until now experienced the most multifaceted foreign influence without a reciprocating effect. By means of this association, the harsh severity of the original national character is increasingly effaced and finally almost entirely destroyed. In its place steps a general European character, and the history of every national poetry of the moderns contains nothing else but the gradual transition from its original character to the subsequent[17] character of an artificial culture [*Bildung*]. Yet already in the earliest ages the different original peculiarities have so much in *common* that they appear as branches of one stock: similarity of languages, of verse forms, utterly peculiar types of poetry! As long as the fables of the age of knights and Christian legends were the mythology of romantic poetry,[18] the similarity of material and the similarity of the spirit of the representations were so great that national differences were almost lost in the uniformity of the whole. The character of that time was simpler and more homogeneous. Yet even after [227] the form of the European world was completely transformed through a total revolution,[19] and the characters of the different nations became diverse and grew apart with the emergence of the third estate, there remained nonetheless much similarity. This exerted its influence on poetry, not only in the character of those types of art whose reigning spirit is bourgeois life, but also in *shared curiosities.*

Yet these traits can be explained by a shared origin and an outward contact, in short, on the basis of the circumstances. There are, however, other remarkable traits of modern poetry, by means of which it decisively distinguishes itself from all other poetries that history has taught us of, and whose ground and purpose can only be deduced satisfactorily out of a common *inner principle.* To this belongs the extremely characteristic steadfastness with which all European nations have pursued the *imitation of the art of antiquity.* Indeed, they have not been deterred entirely by failure; they often return to it anew. The *relation of theory to praxis* is a strange one: for taste itself (in the person of the artist as well as the public) demands of science not only an explanation of its edicts and elucidation of its laws, but it also wants to be pointed in *the right direction;* it wants to have the goal, the direction, and law of art determined. Being at odds with itself and without inner fortitude, diseased taste takes refuge in the prescriptions of a doctor or a quack, even if he can only deceive ingenuousness itself by means of a dictatorial presumption. Add to this the *decisive contrast between a higher and lower art.* Especially now there exist in close proximity to one another two different poetries, each of which has its own [95M] public, and each of which goes its own course unconcerned for the other. They [228] do not take the slightest notice of each other—other than expressing mutual contempt and scorn whenever they accidentally meet one another. And they are often not without secret envy of the popularity of the one or the distinction of the other. The public, which satisfies itself with coarser fare, is naive enough to dismiss all poetry that makes higher claims as being fit only for scholars, extraordinary individuals, or appropriate only for rare, solemn occasions.[20] Furthermore, the *total predominance of the characteristic, individual, and the interesting* is evident throughout modern poetry, especially in more recent ages. Finally, there is the *restless, insatiable striving after something new, piquant, and striking* despite which, however, longing persists unappeased.

When the national elements of modern poetry are torn out of their context and considered as separate and autonomous wholes they are inexplicable. They acquire only from each other substance and meaning. The more carefully one considers the entirety of modern poetry, the more it appears as the mere *piece of a whole*. The *unity* that joins so many common characteristics to a whole is not immediately apparent in the span of its history. We must, accordingly, seek its unity beyond its borders. Modern poetry itself gives us an indication where we should direct our course. The common traits, which appear to be traces of inner interrelation, are less often traits of modern poetry [229] than indications of efforts that have been undertaken and shared circumstances. The similarity of some traits become greater the further we draw back from our own age and the closer we come to others. Thus we must search after their unity in a *twofold* manner; we must turn backward toward the initial *origin* of its genesis and evolution and forward toward the ultimate *objective* of its progression. Perhaps in this way we will succeed in completely explaining its history and in satisfactorily deducing not only the *basis*, but also the *purpose* of its character.

Nothing contradicts the character and even the concept of mankind as much as the idea of a completely isolated force that could function through itself and only in itself. No one will deny that man—at least man as we know him—could exist only in one world. Already the indefinite concept that joins [96M] usual language usage with the words "culture, evolution, development" ["*Kultur, Entwicklung, Bildung*"] presupposes *two different natures*. It presupposes one nature that is formed [*gebildet*] and another that induces and modifies, promotes, and hinders development [*Bildung*] by means of the situation and outward circumstance. Man cannot be active without developing [*bilden*] himself. Development [*Bildung*] is the actual content of every human life and the true object of that nobler history that[21] seeks the necessary in the mutable. As man enters existence, he comes into conflict with fate; his entire life is a constant life-and-death *struggle* with the awesome power from whose arms he can never flee. He is closely surrounded by it on all sides. It does not release him for a moment. One could compare the history of humanity, which sums up the necessary genesis and progression of the development [*Bildung*] of humanity, to military histories. It is the faithful record of the war between humanity and [230] fate. Man does not only need a world outside of himself that can in turn become the impetus, element, and then organ of his activity. Even in the center of his own essence, his enemy—nature, which is set in opposition to him—has established roots. It has often been noted: humanity is a variety of hermaphrodite, an ambiguous mixture of divinity and animality. Humanity has correctly sensed that it is its eternal, necessary character to unify in itself the indissoluble contradictions, the incomprehensible enigma that emerges out of the joining together of what is eternally opposed. The mixed nature of man is comprised of his pure self and a foreign essence. He can never truly settle accounts with fate; he can never definitely say: that is yours, this is mine. Only the mind that has been sufficiently worked upon by fate has the uncommon fortune of being able to be independent. The foundation of his proudest works is often only a gift of nature, and his best deeds are often only half his. Without freedom it would not be a deed: without any external assistance it would not be a human deed. The force to be formed here must necessarily be able to appropriate for itself the capabilities of the formative [*bildenden*] force, and to determine itself at the instigation of this formative force. It must be *free*. The *development* [*Bildung*] or evolution of freedom is the necessary result of all human activity and suffering, the ultimate result of every interaction between freedom and nature. In the reciprocal influence, the constant reciprocal determination that occurs between the two, one of the two forces must necessarily be the active, the other the reactive. Either freedom or nature must give human development the first determining impetus, and thereby determine the direction of the course, the law of the progression, and ultimate goal of its entire trajectory. [97M] This is true regardless if one is considering the evolution of all of humanity or merely an individual, essential component of it. In the first case, the development [*Bildung*] can be termed *natural;* in the latter, *artificial.* In the former, the first original source of activity is a vague longing; in the latter, a specific purpose. In the one, the understanding, despite the utmost cultivation [*Ausbildung*], is at the most only the dogsbody and spokesman of the inclina- [231] tions. Yet the composite drive as a whole is the absolute legislator and director of development [*Bildung*]. Here the drive is also the motive, active power. In the other, the understanding is the guiding, *legislative power:* it is essentially a supreme, *guiding principle* that leads and directs the brute force, determines its direction, specifies the organization of the whole and arbitrarily separates and joins the individual parts.

Experience teaches us that praxis precedes theory in all realms, in every age, in every nation, and in every part of human development [*Bildung*]—and that its formation [*Bildung*] found its origins in nature. Reason can determine a priori that the cause precedes that which is caused, the action the reaction, that the impetus of nature precedes the self-determination of humanity. Art can only follow nature; an artificial culturation [*Bildung*] can only follow a natural culturation [*Bildung*]. In fact, it can only follow an *unsuccessful* natural culturation [*Bildung*]: for if man could progress without difficulty to his goal on the easy path of nature, the assistance of art would be unnecessary and it would, in fact, not be clear what should induce him to strike a new path. The motive force will move itself further in the direction taken if it is not given a new direction by a change in its surroundings. Nature will remain the guiding principle of culturation [*Bildung*] until it has *lost* this right; and probably only an unfortunate misuse of its power would enable man to *displace it from its office*. That the experiment of natural culturation [*Bildung*] could fail is, however, not an improbable premise: the drive is, in fact, a powerful motivator but a blind leader. Moreover, something foreign is at work in the legislating itself: for the drive is not entirely pure; it is put together out of humanity and animality. Artificial culturation [*Bildung*], however, *can* at the least lead to a proper legislation, an enduring perfection and an ultimate, complete satisfaction. This is because the same force that determines the goal of the whole determines as well the direction of the trajectory that guides and organizes the individual parts.

[232]

[98M]

Already in the earliest ages of European culture [*Bildung*] there are to be found the unmistakable traces of the *artificial origins* of modern poetry. The force, the content, was indeed provided by nature: the guiding principle of aesthetic development [*Bildung*] was, however, not the drive but, rather, certain *governing concepts.*[22] Even the individual character of these concepts was caused by the circumstances and necessarily determined by the outward situation. By means of a spontaneous act of the mind, man determines himself according to these concepts, organizes the material at hand, and determines the direction his vitality will take. This act, however, is the original source, the first determining impetus of artificial culturation [*Bildung*],[23] which is attributed, with all due justice, to freedom. The *wild fancy* of romantic poetry, unlike Oriental bombast, does not have an aberrant natural disposition for its foundation. It is, rather, by means of bizarre concepts that fantasy—which is in and of itself felicitous and well disposed toward to beauty—has taken[24] a wrong direction. It stood thus under the rule of concepts, and as feeble and obscure as these might have been, the understanding[25] was the guiding principle of aesthetic development [*Bildung*]. The colossal work of *Dante,* that sublime phenomenon in the cold night of that stern age, is a recent index of the artificial character of the oldest modern poetry. In the particulars no one will mistake the great traits that are to be found throughout it and that could only have

[233]

emanated forth from that natural vitality that can be neither taught nor learned. However, the willful ordering of the whole, the very strange structure of the entire enormous work, we owe not to the divine bard, not to the wise artist but, rather, to the Gothic concepts of the barbarian. *Rhyme* itself appears as a trait of this original artificiality of our aesthetic development [*Bildung*]. [234] The pleasure of the regular repetition of a similar sound perhaps finds its basis in the nature of human sensibility. Every sound of a living being has its own [99M] peculiar meaning; moreover, the similarity of many sounds is not without meaning. Just as the individual sound denotes the transitory situation, so does this repetition denote an enduring peculiarity. It is the resounding characteristic, the musical portrait of a particular organization.[26] Thus many kinds of animals repeat the same sound in order to inform the world of their identity— they rhyme. One could also imagine that—due to an unfavorable or extremely aberrant natural disposition—a people could genuinely take great pleasure in the similarity of sounds.[27] Yet only where false concepts determined the direction of poetic development [*Bildung*] could one elevate a strange Gothic finery to a necessary law and the childish pleasure in capricious frivolity to the ultimate purpose of art. Precisely because of this primordial barbarism of rhyme it is an extremely rare and difficult art to deal with properly. The admirable skill of the greatest master is barely adequate to make it harmless. In [235] fine art rhyme will always be a strange disruption. It demands rhythm and melody: for only the uniform similarity of the twofold quantity of successive sounds can express the universal.[28] The regular similarity in the physical quality of many sounds can only express the *individual*.[29] In the hand of a great master it can undeniably acquire much meaning and become an important organ of *characteristic* poetry. In this regard also the result confirms that rhyme (next to the rule of the characteristic itself) is most properly at home in the artificial development [*Bildung*] of poetry.

It should not puzzle us that, in comparison to later times, there are few traces of artificiality in the beginnings of modern poetry. The great barbarian intermezzo—which occupies the space between ancient and modern culture [*Bildung*]—first had to be brought to an end before the character of the latter could become prominent. There remained enough fragments of the peculiar traits of antiquity; yet by means of the national individuality of the Nordic victors a fresh branch was grafted onto the decayed trunk. Of course, nature in its fledgling state first had to have time to become, to grow, and to develop before art could arbitrarily guide it and test its own inexperience on it. The *seed* of artificial culturation [*Bildung*] had been present for some time: in an artifi- [236] cial universal religion;[30] in the inexpressible misery that was the final result of the necessary decadence of natural culturation [*Bildung*]; in the many skills, inventions, and forms of knowledge that were not lost. What was still present

[100M]   from the harvest of former ages was available to the barbaric new-
comers. It was a great and rich inheritance, which they paid dearly for in that
the most extreme immorality of a self-absorbed nature was at the same time
passed on! The earth first had to be reclaimed and cultivated before this seed
could gradually develop and before the new form could gradually step into the
light out of the womb of barbarism. Moreover, the modern spirit—what with
the requisite needs of religion and politics—had so much to manage that only
later could it think of the luxury of beauty. For this reason, European poetry
remained for some time almost entirely national.[31] Other than its natural
character only a few unmistakable and yet rare traces of the artificial character
are visible.

Indeed, governing concepts exert their influence on aesthetic praxis: they
themselves, however, are so feeble that they could at the most be taken for the
early traces of a future theory. There exists as of yet no actual theory that could
be separated from praxis and that would be to some extent coherent. Later on,
however, *theory* steps forward with its large entourage all the more hungry for
domination, reaches ever further around it, announces itself as the legislative
[237]   principle of modern poetry and is furthermore acknowledged as such by the
public as well as by artists and experts. Its great objective would be to restore to
corrupted taste the legitimacy it has lost and to restore to an art gone astray its
true direction. Yet theory could generally be accepted only when it is universally valid. Only then could it raise itself from an impotent presumptuousness
to the rank of a truly public power. That theory up until now has hardly been
what it should be is already apparent in that it could never come to agreement
with itself. Until this point the boundaries between understanding and feeling
in the realm of art must be transgressed continually from both sides. A theory
that is biased will presume greater rights than would accrue to even a universally valid theory. Decadent taste, however, will impart its own improper
orientation to science instead of receiving a better orientation from it. Dulled
or base feelings, confused or distorted judgments, incomplete or commonplace
intuitions will not only produce a great deal of individual incorrect concepts
and principles but also give rise to fundamentally inappropriate paths of inquiry, utterly wrong principles. Hence the bifurcated character of modern
theory, which is the undeniable result of its entire history. It is, namely, in part a
[101M]   true reflection of modern taste, the distilled concept of an incorrect praxis, the
rule of barbarism, and in part the commendable, constant striving for a universally valid science.

All—even the strangest—aspects of modern poetry can be explained
entirely by this predominance of the understanding, by this artificiality of our
aesthetic development [*Bildung*].

During the childhood of the governing understanding, when the theorizing instinct is not capable of issuing forth out of itself a self-sufficient product, it is in the habit of pursuing a *given intuition* when it has the *presentiment* of universality—which is the object of all its efforts. Hence the conspicuous *imitation of the ancients* to which all European nations so early took recourse, and in which they persevere with the most steadfast tenacity and to which, after a short pause, they always return anew. For the theorizing instinct hoped especially here to be successful in its efforts to discover the objectivity it sought. The childish understanding elevates the individual example to a general rule, ennobles tradition, and sanctions prejudice. The *authority of the ancients* (indeed, as badly one understood them, so wrongly did one imitate them) is the fundamental law in the constitution of the oldest aesthetic dogmatism, which was, in turn, only the rehearsal for a truly philosophical theory of poetry. [238]

The arbitrariness of the governing principle of development is boundless; the *separation* and *mixture* of all the materials and forces present at hand comprise the dangerous tools its inexperience employs. Without suspecting what it is doing, it pursues a course characterized by a destructive inequity. Its first attempt is a mistake that brings countless others with it, which the effort of many centuries can hardly make good again. The absurd constraints of its foolish laws, and its forcible divisions and combinations circumscribe, disorder, obscure, and finally destroy nature. The works that it produces lack an inner principle of life; they are only individual pieces bound together by an external force, without any actual interrelation. They do not make a whole. After various efforts, the resulting fruit of its extensive labor is often nothing else than a thorough[32] anarchy, a complete lack of character. The general mixture of national characters, the constant reciprocal imitation throughout modern poetry, could be explained by the political and religious interrelation of a population that was very affected by its outward circumstance and that originated from a common lineage: nonetheless it acquires by means of the artificiality of culturation [*Bildung*] an entirely peculiar cast. With natural culturation [*Bildung*] at least certain limits of segregation as well as unification would be distinct and certain. Only the arbitrariness of intention could produce such a boundless confusion[33] and eradicate finally every trace of law-governedness![34] Indeed, there are still always as many conglomerations of peculiarities as there are great cultivated nations. Yet the few common traits that exist are very tenuous, and actually every artist exists unto himself, an *isolated egoist* in the midst of his age and his people. There are as many individual mannerisms as there are original artists. The richest variety accompanies mannered tendentiousness as soon as the aroused force of nature, under the pressure of artificial [239] [102M] constraint, begins to unleash its abundance. For the more distant one is from the unsullied truth, the more biased views there are of it. The greater the body of original works that already exists, the more infrequent will be every new work of genuine originality. For this reason there are countless legions of derivative imitators [*Echokünstler*]. Hence brilliant originality is the ultimate goal of the artist and the highest criterion of the expert.

[240] Understanding can indeed, at the high price of countless errors, finally attain a belated and more accurate insight and then safely approximate an enduring perfection. It is thus unarguably possible that it could rightfully—in the name of a higher purpose—change, efface, and even destroy the original national character. Far more infelicitous, however, are its chemical[35] experiments in the arbitrary division and mixture of the original arts and the pure types of art. Unavoidably, its infelicitous acumen will violently wreak havoc on nature, falsify its simplicity, and essentially disperse and destroy its beautiful organization into elementary masses. It is extremely uncertain if new combinations and types can be discovered by means of these artificial assemblages. How can the boundaries of the individual arts not be confused in the unification of several art forms? In one and the same work of art poetry is often both the despot and slave of music. The poet wants to portray what only the actor is capable of; and he leaves gaps for the actor that only he himself could fill. Only the genre of drama could offer us a rich collection of examples of the unnatural combinations of the pure types of art. I select a single but nonetheless shining example: the monstrosity of the genre becomes all the more visible by means of the excellence of the execution.[36] There is a type of modern drama that one could call *lyric*. Not because of individual lyric parts: for every beautiful drama-

[241] tic totality is put together out of nothing but lyrical elements. Rather, it is a poem in dramatic form whose unity is a musical mood or a lyrical

[103M] uniformity—the dramatic expression of a lyric enthusiasm. Because the unity of the mood can not be grasped by means of the understanding, but can only be apprehended by means of a more refined sensibility, no genre is so often and to such an extent misconstrued by incompetent experts as this one. One of the most excellent poems of this type, Shakespeare's *Romeo,* is essentially but a romantic sigh over the fleeting brevity of youthful joy, a beautiful lament that these freshest of blossomings in the spring of life wither away so quickly under the callous breath of harsh fate. It is an enchanting *elegy,* where sweet agony is indissolubly bound up with the painful pleasure of the most delicate love. This bewitching mixture of indissolubly intertwined grace and pain is, however, precisely the true character of the elegy.

Nothing can better explain and confirm the artificiality of modern aesthetic development [*Bildung*] than the great *predominance of the individual, the characteristic, and the philosophical* throughout the entire mass of modern poetry. The numerous and outstanding works of art, whose goal is a philosophical interest, do not simply form [*bilden*] an insignificant secondary type of the poetic arts; they form, rather, an entirely distinct major genre that divides into two subsidiary types. There is a self-sufficient representation of the individual and general, of conditioned and unconditioned knowledge, which is as distinct from fine art as it is from science and history. The ugly is often indispensable to its completion, and it uses even beauty only as a means to its specific, philosophical purpose. In general, the realm of the representational arts has been too narrowly restricted and that of fine art too far extended.[37] The *specific character* of fine art is a free play without determined goal;[38] that of the representational   [242] arts in general is the ideality of representation. A representation (be its organ description or imitation) in which the represented material is chosen and ordered and, if possible, formed according to the laws of the representing spirit is *ideal*. If it is permissible to designate as *artists* all those whose medium is ideal representation, whose goal, however, is the absolutely unconditioned, then there are three specific, different classes of artists; each is distinguished according to whether their goal is the good, beauty, or the truth. There are insights that cannot be imparted by means of historical imitation or intellectual description but can only be presented as individual, ideal intuitions, as examples and instances of concepts and ideas. However, there are also works of art— ideal representations—which apparently have no other goal than knowledge. Ideal poetry, whose goal is the philosophically interesting, I term *didactic*   [104M] *poetry*.[39] Works whose subject matter is didactic but whose purpose is aesthetic—or works whose subject matter and purpose are didactic, yet whose outer form is poetic—should not be termed didactic: for the individual qualities of the subject matter can never be a sufficient principle for an adequate, aesthetic classification.[40] The tendency of most excellent and famous modern poems is philosophical. Indeed, modern poetry appears here to have   [243/105M] attained a certain perfection, an ultimate of its kind. The didactic class is its pride and its virtue; it is its most original product, affected neither out of distorted imitation nor out of mistaken doctrine but, rather, produced out of the hidden depths of its natural vitality.   [244]

The wide compass of the characteristic evident throughout the aesthetic development [*Bildung*] of the moderns reveals itself also in other arts. Is there not a characteristic *pictorial art*, whose interest is neither aesthetic nor historical but, rather, purely *physiognomical* and hence philosophical, whose treatment, however, is not historical but ideal? It infinitely surpasses poetry in specificity of individuality just as it is surpassed by it in compass, coherence, and completeness. Even in *music* that which is characteristic in individual objects gains the upper hand despite the nature of this art. The characteristic also rules absolutely in the *dramatic arts*. A virtuoso of mimicry must—in terms of organiza-

[245]   tion and spirit—be a physical and intellectual Proteus in order to metamorphize himself into every style and into every character so that he incorporates
even the most individual traits. In the course of which beauty is neglected,
propriety is often offended, and the mimic rhythm is entirely forgotten.[41]

What was more natural than that the guiding principle also became the
legislating principle? that the philosophically interesting became the ultimate
goal of poetry? The prescinding understanding begins by dividing and
dismembering the whole of nature. Thus under its guidance art orients itself
entirely toward the faithful imitation of the particular. With greater intellectual
development [*Bildung*], the goal of modern poetry naturally becomes *individuality* that is *original and interesting.* The simple imitation of the particular is,
however, a mere skill of the *copyist,* not a free art. Only by means of an
arrangement that is *ideal* does the characteristic of an individual become a
philosophical work of art. As a result of being organized in such a manner, the
law of the whole must clearly emerge from the sum total and effortlessly offer
itself to inspection; the meaning, spirit, and inner coherence of the represented
essence must come forth out of it. Thus even characteristic poetry can and
should represent the general within the particular; yet this generality (which is
the goal of the whole and the principle of the organization of the sum total) is
not aesthetic; rather, it is didactic. But even the most comprehensive philo-
[106M]   sophical characteristic is only one salient point for the understanding; it is a
conditioned knowledge, a piece of a whole that does not satisfy reason's striv-
[246]   ing. The instinct of reason constantly strives for a perfect completeness in itself,
and strides incessantly from the conditioned to the unconditioned. The demand for unconditionality and completeness is the origin and ground of the
second type of the didactic genre. This is the true *philosophical poetry,* which is
of interest not only to the understanding but to reason as well. Its own natural
evolution and progression leads characteristic poetry to *philosophical tragedy,*
which is the complete opposite of aesthetic tragedy. Consisting of nothing but
lyrical elements, the former is the culmination of the poetic arts—it results
ultimately in the utmost harmony. Consisting of nothing but characteristic
elements, the latter is the greatest work of art of didactic poetry—it results
ultimately in the utmost disharmony.[42] Its catastrophe is tragic; this is not true
of it in its entirety: for the thorough purity of the tragic (which is a necessary
precondition of aesthetic tragedy) would harm the truth of characteristic and
philosophical art.

This is not the place to set forth in a thorough manner the as of yet
entirely unknown theory of philosophical tragedy. Yet hopefully it is acceptable
to explain the concept set forth here of this type of poetry—which is itself such
an interesting phenomenon in addition to being one of the most important
documents for the characterization of modern poetry—by means of a single

example, which remains, in content and the complete interrelation of the whole, the most outstanding of its kind. *Hamlet* is so poorly understood that it [247] is only praised in parts. Which is rather illogical, if the whole is truly so incoherent, so senseless, as is tacitly presupposed! In Shakespeare's dramas in general the interrelation is so simple and clear that it openly and impartially illuminates the meaning visibly and from itself. The ground of the interrelation, however, is often so deeply hidden, the invisible bonds, the relations, are so subtle that even the most astute critical analysis must fail if discrimination is lacking, if one brings false expectations or proceeds from false principles. In *Hamlet* all individual parts necessarily develop out of a common center and react in turn on it. Nothing is extraneous, superfluous, or coincidental in this masterpiece of artistic wisdom.[43] The center of the whole lies in the character of the hero. By means of a remarkable situation all the might of his noble [107M] nature is concentrated in the understanding; the active force, however, is entirely destroyed. His mind pulls itself in different directions as if it were on a torture rack; it disintegrates and perishes in the surfeit of futile understanding that oppresses it even more profoundly than all those that approximate it. There is perhaps no more perfect representation than the character of *Hamlet* [248] of the indissoluble disharmony that is the actual object of philosophical tragedy[44]—that is to say, a limitless disparity between the thinking and active force—as in Hamlet's character. The overall impression of this tragedy is that of a *maximum of despair*. All impressions, which by themselves appear great and important, disappear nonetheless as trivial before that which discloses itself as the ultimate and solitary result of all being and thought, before the eternal *colossal dissonance* that ceaselessly separates humanity and fate.

In the entire realm of modern poetry this drama is one of the most important documents for the historian of aesthetics. In it the spirit of its author [249] is most in evidence; here what is scattered and isolated in other works is gathered together. Of all artists, however, *Shakespeare* is the one who most completely and accurately characterizes the spirit of modern poetry in general. In him the charming blossomings of romantic fantasy and the enormous magnitude of the Gothic age of heroes are united with the finest traits of modern social life and the most profound and the most comprehensive poetic philosophy.[45] In the last two regards it could appear at times as if he had anticipated the culture [*Bildung*] of our age. Who excels him in the inexhaustible wealth of the interesting? In the energy of passions of all kinds? In the inimitable truth of the characteristic? In unique originality? He encompasses the most peculiar aesthetic merits of the moderns in their fullest range, in their utmost perfection—and in their utmost peculiarity, including even the eccen- [108M] tric oddities and failings attendant on them. Without exaggeration, one can call him the *pinnacle of modern poetry*. How replete he is in individual beauties of every kind! How often does he come extremely close to the truly unattainable! In the whole of modern poetry nothing corresponds to complete beauty so much as the charming grandeur that has been perfected to the point of grace in the character of *Brutus* in *Caesar*.

Nonetheless, many learned and acute thinkers do not really know what to do with Shakespeare. Such an "incorrect" person did not want to accept their conventional theories. An irresistible sympathy befriends the expert that lacks sensitivity and a keen eye with respectable poets who are too weak to be capable of excesses. It is thus not much more than the mediocrity of those artists—who are altogether tepid—that has been certified and made sacrosanct under the name of *correctness*. The typical judgment that Shakespeare's incorrectness sins against the rules of art is, at the least, very premature as long as no objective theory about art exists. Moreover, there has hardly been any theoretician who has even attempted to develop more completely the rules of characteristic poetry and philosophical art. It is true that Shakespeare has, despite the constant protestations about orderliness, always irresistibly enthralled the masses. Yet I doubt whether his philosophical spirit could actually be comprehensible to the masses. Swept up by his sensual force, stirred by his deceptive truths, and enchanted to the utmost by his inexhaustible abundance, it was perhaps only the *physical mass* of his works that checked them.

[250]

It seems that we have entirely lost the proper perspective. Whoever judges his poetry to be *beautiful* art,[46] will—the more discrimination he possesses and the better he knows the poet—only end up with more profound contradictions. Just as nature produces the beautiful and ugly mixed together and with the same luxuriant abundance, so does Shakespeare. None of his dramas are beautiful *in their entirety;* beauty never determines the arrangement of the whole. As in nature, even the particular beautiful elements are only rarely free of *ugly adjuncts;* they are only the *means* to another purpose. They serve the characteristic or philosophical interest. He is often also awkward and uncouth where a more subtle refinement was close at hand—precisely for the sake of greater interest. His abundance is often an indissoluble confusion and the result of the whole an endless strife. Even in the midst of the merriest figures of uninhibited childhood or joyful youth, a bitter memory of the utter purposelessness of life, of the complete emptiness of all existence wounds us. Nothing is so revolting, bitter, outrageous, disgusting, uninspired, and hideous, that he would not depict it as soon as he sees a purpose to it. He often *flays* his subjects, and digs as if with an anatomical knife in the revolting decay of moral corpses. It is a far too exaggerated mitigation to say "that it makes man acquainted with his fate in the most genial manner." Actually, one can't even say that he leads us to a *pure* truth. He presents us with only a *one-sided* view of

[251]

[109M]

truth—admittedly, the richest and most comprehensive view. His representation is never objective; rather, it is thoroughly *mannered*.[47] although I am the first to admit that his style is the greatest, and his individuality the most interesting that we know of as of yet. It has often been remarked that the original character of his individual style is unmistakable and inimitable. Perhaps the individual can only be individually understood and represented. Characteristic art and style at least seem to be inseparable companions, necessary correlates. By style in art I understand an individual orientation of spirit and an individual disposition of sensibility, which expresses itself in representations that should be ideal.[48] [252]

The[49] general orientation of poetry—indeed, the whole aesthetic development [*Bildung*] of modernity—toward the interesting can be explained by this lack of universality, this rule of the mannered, characteristic, and individual.[50] Every original individual[51] that contains a greater quantity of intellectual content or aesthetic energy is *interesting*. I said deliberately: *greater*. [253] Greater, namely, than the receptive individual already possess: for the interesting demands an individual receptiveness, indeed, often a momentarily individual mood. Since all magnitudes can be multiplied into infinity, it is clear why a complete satisfaction can never be attained in this way, why there can be no *endpoint* when it comes to the *interesting*. Throughout the most varied forms and orientations, in all degrees of vitality, the same *need for a complete satisfaction,* a consistent striving for *an absolute maximum of art* expresses itself in all [110M] modern poetry. What theory promised, what one sought in nature, what one hoped to find in each idol—what was this but a *ne plus ultra* of the *aesthetic?* The more often the longing for a complete satisfaction that would be grounded in human nature was disappointed by the individual and mutable, the more ardent and restless it became. Only the universally valid, enduring, and necessary—the *objective*—can fill this great gap; only the beautiful can still this ardent yearning. *Beauty* (the concept of which I put forth as problematic, and leave its actual validity and applicability for now as undecided) is the universally valid object of an uninterested pleasure, which, independent of the constraint of needs and laws, is at the same time independent, free, and necessary, entirely purposeless and yet unconditionally purposeful. The predominance of the individual leads of its own accord to the objective; the interesting is the propaedeutic for the beautiful, and the ultimate goal of modern poetry can be nothing else than the *ne plus ultra of beauty,* a maximum of objective aesthetic perfection.

In this second point of contact, all the different streams into which [254] modern poetry has divided itself since its origins meet together anew. The explanation for its attributes is to be found in the artificiality of its development

[*Bildung*]. If the direction and goal of its trajectory makes comprehensible *the goal of its striving*, then the meaning of the whole will be explained fully and our question answered.

The predominance of the interesting is simply a mere *passing crisis* of taste: for it must finally annihilate itself. Yet the two catastrophes from which it has to choose are very different from one another. If the trend verges more toward aesthetic energy, taste—accustomed more and more to the old pleasures—will increasingly desire intenser and keener pleasures. It will pass over quickly enough into piquancy and the astonishing. *Piquancy* is what desperately stimulates a dulled sensibility; the *astonishing* is a similar stimulus for the imagination. These are the harbingers of a near death. The *jejune* is the meager nourishment of the impotent; and the *shocking*—be it bizarre, disgusting, or horrible—is the last convulsion of a dying[52] taste.[53] If, however,

[IIIM]
[255]

philosophical content predominates in the orientation of taste, and nature is strong enough not to succumb to the most violent convulsions, the striving force—after it has exhausted itself in the production of an excessive abundance of the interesting—will forcibly brace itself and move on to attempts at objectivity. Hence genuine taste in our age is neither a gift of nature nor a result of culture [*Bildung*] alone; rather, only a great ethical vitality and an established autonomy make it possible.

The sublime objective [*Bestimmung*] of modern poetry is thus nothing less than the highest goal of every possible poetry; it is the utmost that can be demanded of art; it is the utmost art can strive toward. That which is unconditionally the *ne plus ultra*, however, can never be entirely attained. The utmost that the striving force can attain is more and more to approximate this unattainable goal. And even this *endless approximation* does not seem to be without inner contradictions—which make its possibility doubtful. The return from decadent art to genuine art, from corrupted taste to correct taste, appears to be achievable only through a *sudden leap*—which in turn does not allow itself to be combined with the *constant progression* by means of which every skill tends to develop. That which is objective is immutable and enduring: should art and[54] taste ever attain objectivity, aesthetic development [*Bildung*] would accordingly have to be *fixed*. An *absolute cessation* of aesthetic development [*Bildung*] is inconceivable. Accordingly, modern poetry will always change. But can it not just as well move *backward* away from the goal? Can it not still do this even if it has taken a more appropriate direction? Are not all human endeavors

[256]

futile?[55] Already in particular instances beauty is an act of goodwill on the part of nature. How much more will the whole always depend on a particular confluence of unique circumstances, which man could never be able to direct, let alone bring forth? In general, so it would seem, one can never be moderate enough when it comes to the claims about the self-sufficiency of the whole. Its development [*Bildung*], its progression, and its ultimate success remain—what an unfortunate lot!—left to *coincidence.*

All men of a better sort hate coincidence and all that is attendant upon it in every form. The great task of fate must essentially be a summons to attentiveness and activity for all who interest themselves in poetry. Even if there is little hope and the solution is difficult: *the attempt is necessary!* Whoever remains indifferent and lazy does not care for the dignity of art and humanity. What use   [112M] are the achievements of culture [*Bildung*] without a secure foundation? What use is vitality without a sure direction, without proportion and balance? What use is a chaos of particular beautiful elements without a complete, pure beauty? Only the certain prospect of a beneficent catastrophe in the future could assuage and reassure us about the current condition of aesthetic development [*Bildung*].

It is true that the course of modern culturation [*Bildung*], the spirit of our age—especially the German national character—do not seem favorably disposed toward poetry! "How tasteless," many could perhaps think, "are all our institutions and opinions, how unpoetic are all practices, indeed, the entire way of life of the moderns! Everywhere there rules impassioned confusion, ugly strife, and an awkward formality that lacks life and spirit. In vain I search for a liberal abundance, a graceful unity. Does this mean one misconstrues the noble vitality of the ancestors of the Germans, when one entertains doubts as to whether the Goths were born poets? Or whether even the barbaric Christianity   [257] of the monks was a beautiful religion? A thousand proofs proclaim unanimously to you: *prose* is the true nature of the moderns. Earlier there was at least tremendous vitality and fantastic life in modern poetry. Soon, however, art became the scholarly plaything of conceited virtuosos. The life force of that heroic age was thus extinguished, the spirit flown; only the echo of the earlier significance remained. What is the poetry of the subsequent age but a chaos of wretched fragments of romantic poetry, abortive imitations of misunderstood models, and impotent attempts at absolute perfection—which fly straight toward heaven with waxen wings? Thus barbarians patched together Gothic buildings out of fragments of a better world. Thus the Nordic student laboriously completes with strict discipline lifeless paintings after the fashion of antiquity! Humanity blossomed only once and never will again. Fine art was this blossoming. In the bitter of winter no artificial spring allows itself to be forced. Moreover, the general spirit of the age is dissipated weariness and amorality. You are wretched and yet want to appear beautiful? Your innards are riddled with worms and yet your outward appearance should be pure? What a senseless undertaking! Where the character is emasculated, where there is no actual ethical development [*Bildung*], art naturally sinks to the base frisson of a

[258]   dissipated opulence. The fate of German poetry is the most hopeless! Among
          the English and French the representation of social life at least has an original
          truth, a permanence, a living sense, and a genuine meaning. The German,
          however, cannot depict what he does not have; when he attempts this he falls
[113M]   into strained reveries or into aloofness. It is indeed true that the awkward
          uncouthness, the dull melancholy, and the resolute stubbornness of the En-
          glish, and the superficial intensity, the shallow impetuousness, the refined
          vacuity, and the biased national character of the French keep them far enough
          away from perfect beauty. The narrow-minded tediousness, the confused cum-
          bersomeness, the age-old deliberate sluggishness of its spirit makes the charac-
          terless German utterly incapable of the graceful play of free art. Particular
          exceptions do not prove anything about the whole. If one finds here and there
          signs of taste in Germany, so what—there were Romans under Nero, too."

          In such, and even darker, historical portraits à la Rembrandt does one
          with hellish colors depict—not without a festive pathos in execution, admit-
          tedly, but actually with a decided carelessness—the spirit of great peoples, the
          spirit of a remarkable age. Each particular trait of this representation may be
          true, or may contain something truthful; yet if the traits are not complete, if the
          context is missing, then the whole is false. In the context of our age, the greatest
          aesthetic langorousness is clearly a *favorable symptom* of the passing beneficent
          crisis of the interesting to which only a weak nature succumbs. This languor
          originates out of the most violent and often overstrained striving; for this
          reason the most exuberant vitality is so often close at hand. The decline is
          naturally commensurate with the extent of, and the toll exacted by, the exer-
          tion. The lack of ethics may be true of the whole, yet it would seriously hinder
          that progress of taste, which could in turn easily foster ethical development
          [*Bildung*]. Taste is to a much greater extent free of external compulsion and
          pernicious contagion. The ethical development [*Bildung*] of even the particular
          is much more easily swept up by the seductive power of the whole, suppressed
          by all-prevailing prejudices, fettered by outward circumstances of every kind.
          Whether the poetry of the moderns will attain its highest determination or not
[259]   cannot depend solely on a providential national character: for its development
          [*Bildung*] is artificial. The more refined taste of the moderns should not be a
          gift of nature; rather, it should be an independent attainment based on the
          freedom they enjoy. If strength is present, then art will finally be able to rectify
          the one-sided taste of the moderns and to take the place of the greatest benev-
          olence of nature. The moderns are not lacking in *aesthetic vitality,* even if sage
          guidance is lacking. One can certainly defend their poetic disposition. Indeed,
          nature has not been stingy with the Italians. There are among the Germans
[114M]   enough reminders left that attest that German taste was formed later on. As
          much as they surpass the other cultivated nations of Europe in particulars, the

Germans lag behind them in the whole. Unassuming inventiveness and modest force are the original characteristic traits of this nation, which often misjudges itself. The notorious German *obsession to imitate* may now and then deserve the mockery that one tends to denounce it with.[56] On the whole, however, versatility indicates a genuine progression of aesthetic development [*Bildung*] and is a near harbinger of universality. The so-called characterlessness of the Germans is far preferable to the manneristic character of other nations. Only when the national bias of their aesthetic development [*Bildung*] is more attenuated and rectified will they be able to elevate themselves to a higher level of that versatility.

The character of the aesthetic development [*Bildung*] of our age and our nation betrays itself through a remarkable and great symptom. *Goethe's* poetry is [260] the dawning of a genuine art and pure beauty. The sensuous vigor that was to inspire an age, a people, was only the least of the exceptional qualities that characterized the young Goethe. The philosophical content, the characteristic truth of his subsequent works can be compared to the inexhaustible wealth of Shakespeare. Indeed, if *Faust* were to be completed, it would probably surpass *Hamlet,* the Englishman's masterpiece, whose goal it appears to share. What in *Hamlet* is only fate and circumstance—in other words, weakness—is in *Faust* mind and action—in other words, vitality. Hamlet's mood and manner are a result of his outward circumstances; Faust's similar manner is a result of his essential character. The versatility of this poet's ability to represent is so boundless that one could call him the *Proteus* of artists and compare him to that god of the seas of whom it is said:

First was he a lion with frightful flowing mane.
He flowed then as water, and murmured as a tree in the clouds.[57]

One can then excuse the mystic formulation of what is a correct observation, when some enthusiasts attribute a certain *poetic omnipotence* to him and suggest that nothing is impossible for him, and who wear themselves out with astute treatises on his *uniqueness.*

It seems to me that such studied rapture lacks the proper perspective. One does Goethe a great injustice when one metamorphosizes him into a German Shakespeare. When it comes to characteristic poetry the manneristic [115M] Englishman would perhaps still maintain the advantage. The goal of the German, however, is the objective. Beauty is the true measure by which his charm- [261] ing poetry is to be appreciated. What could be more appealing than the graceful gaiety, the quiet mirth of his temper, the unadulterated specificity, the delicate gentleness of his contours? Here there is not simply vitality, but also elegant proportions and equilibrium! The graces themselves disclose to their fondling the secret of a *beautiful arrangement*. Through an agreeable alternation of stillness and movement he is able to spread the most charming life evenly over the whole; and in simple components the liberal abundance orders itself of its own accord into a light, graceful unity.

He stands midway between the interesting and the beautiful, between the mannered and the objective. It should thus not disconcert us that in a few of his works his own individuality becomes too noticeable and that in many others he metamorphizes himself according to whim and assumes foreign mannerisms. These are essentially vestigial remnants of the epoch of the characteristic and individual. And yet he knows how to bring even into mannerism a type of objectivity in as much as this is possible. Thus he indulges himself at times with trivial material, which in turn becomes here and there so meager and unimportant that it seems as if he were seriously involved in producing totally pure poems lacking in all material substance—just as there is empty thought without content. In these works, the drive relevant to the beautiful is essentially otiose: they are a pure product of the representational drive alone. It could almost seem as if the objectivity of his art were not solely an innate talent but, rather, a result of cultivation [*Bildung*]; the beauty of his works, however, seems to be the result of an unintentional adjunct to his original nature. In what is joyful as well as what is moving he is always charming; as often as he wants, he is beautiful; he is seldom purely sublime. Out of impetuous intensity his impassioned strength flits occasionally to the harsh and outrageous, or out of easeful languor to the lackluster. Usually, however, fantastic strength is wedded to a wiser forbearance in the most felicitous manner. Where he is entirely free of mannerism, his depictions are like the peaceful and serene perspective of a nobler spirit that knows no weakness and is disturbed by no suffering but who [262] alone grasps vitality in its purity and presents it for all eternity. Where he is entirely himself, the spirit of his charming poetry is characterized by a *delightful* [116M] *abundance* and an *enchanting grace*.

This great artist opens up a prospect to an entirely *new level of aesthetic development* [*Bildung*]. His works are an irrefutable attestation that the objective is possible and that the hope for the beautiful is not an empty delusion of reason. The *objective* is attained here already. And because the necessary violence of instinct must lead every stronger aesthetic force (that does not wear itself out) out of the crisis of the interesting to the objective, the objective soon becomes more general; it is publically acknowledged, and becomes *all-prevailing*. Then aesthetic development [*Bildung*] has *attained the decisive point*, where, left to itself, it can never wane but can only be halted in its progress through external violence, or completely destroyed by a physical revolution. I mean the great, moral revolution, by means of which freedom in its struggle with fate (within culture [*Bildung*]) finally achieves a decisive advantage over nature. This occurs in the important moment when self-sufficiency comes to prevail in the motive principle, in the strength of the mass; for the guiding principle of artificial culturation [*Bildung*] is already self-sufficient. After this revolution not only will the course of culturation [*Bildung*], the direction of aesthetic force, the organization of the entire mass of communal products determine themselves according to the aim and law of humanity, but humanity will also predominate in the force and mass of culture [*Bildung*] that is at hand. If nature does not receive *sustenance*—as in a physical revolution,[58] which could also, of course, destroy all culture in one blow—humanity can progress in its evolution undisturbed.[59] Artificial culturation [*Bildung*] can at least not recede back *into itself* like natural culturation [*Bildung*]. It is no surprise that, in the course of this hard struggle, freedom finally wins, even if the superiority of nature in the beginning of culturation [*Bildung*] is so great. For man's strength grows with doubled progression, in that every advance not only yields greater forces, but also provides new means to further advances. The guiding understanding may, as long as it is inexperienced, just as often do damage to itself: yet there must come a time when it will more than make amends for all its mistakes. Brute superior strength must finally succumb to the reasonable opponent. Nothing is more self-evident than the theory of perfectibility. The pure principle of reason concerning the necessary, infinite perfection of humanity is fairly straightforward. Yet its application to history—if *vision* is lacking to hit the actual mark, to apprehend the right moment, to survey the whole—can give rise to the worst misunderstandings. It is always difficult, often impossible, to break down the confused web of experience into its simple strands, to properly value the present stage of culturation [*Bildung*], to accurately guess the next stage of culturation [*Bildung*].

Ruling concepts determine the course and direction of modern culture [*Bildung*]. Their influence is extremely important, indeed, decisive. Just as in modernity, where there are only a few fragments of genuine ethical development [*Bildung*], and where moral prejudice instead of noble and good convictions prevails: there are, accordingly, *aesthetic prejudices,* which are far more deeply ingrained, more broadly disseminated, and incomparably more harmful than might appear at first glance. The gradual and slow sequential evolution of the understanding necessarily brings with it biased opinions. These indeed contain particular traits of truth, but the traits are incomplete and ripped out of their actual context. Thus the perspective is distorted and the whole destroyed. Such prejudices are at the same time to a certain extent occasionally useful and have a limited expediency. Thus the striving for the objective was steadfastly sustained by the orthodox belief that there is a science [*Wissenschaft*] that is by itself sufficient to produce beautiful works; and at least the system of aesthetic anarchy served to dismantle the despotism of a biased theory. More dangerous

[263]

[117M]

[264]

and quite reprehensible are other aesthetic prejudices that restrict further evolution itself. It is the most holy duty of all friends of art to fight mercilessly and to eradicate entirely wherever possible such errors, which cajole natural freedom, and cripple independent vitality by presenting the hopes of art as impossible and the efforts it undertakes as fruitless.

Many thus think: "Fine art is not actually the property of all of humanity; least of all is it a result of artificial culturation [*Bildung*]. It is the spontaneous outpouring of a propitious nature, the *local* result of a most fortunate climate, a *momentary epoch,* a passing blossoming—essentially the brief springtime of humanity. There reality itself is already noble, beautiful, and charming; and the most common folk tale is, without any artificial adjustment, enchanting poetry. That fresh blossoming of youthful fantasy, that powerful and supple [118M] elasticity, that greater salutariness of feeling could not be affected; and once it is ruined it can never again be healed. Least of all under the Nordic severity of a somber heaven, the barbarism of a Gothic mindset, the utter detachment of scholarly pedantry."

Perhaps with a great deal of qualification this can be true for at least a portion of fine art. In fact, it appears that, for the plastic arts, the lack of a [265] propitious organization and a favorable climate cannot be replaced by means of a forcible inducement on the part of freedom or by means of the utmost cultivation [*Bildung*].[60] One extends this, unjustly and contrary to all experience, to poetry as well. There are many great bards and fortunate poets, whose natural ardor could not be extinguished through the most severe repression, to be found everywhere. Poetry is a *universal* art.[61] For its organ,[62] *fantasy,* is already incomparably more closely related to freedom, and more independent from external influence. Poetry and poetic taste is thus far more corruptible than[63] plastic taste, but also *infinitely more perfectible.* In any case, the fresh blossoming of youthful fantasy is a priceless gift of nature and at the same time the most fleeting. Even a single poisonous breeze drains its aspect of innocence; and the beautiful flower, wilting, sinks its head. But even when the capacity for fantasy has been stifled and dulled for some time by pedantry and worn out and debilitated by opulence, it can still rouse itself back to life at the inducement of freedom and gradually perfect itself by means of genuine culturation [*Bildung*]. It can indeed attain again strength, fire, elasticity: yet the fresh aspect, the [266] romantic scent of that spring does not return that easily in that autumn.

There is another prejudice that finds wide currency and entirely denies all independent existence, all peculiar permanence, to fine art. Indeed, it entirely denies its specific difference. I fear that if certain people were to think aloud, many voices would express themselves as follows: "Poetry is nothing but the symbolic children's language of a youthful humanity: it is only the *pro-*

padeutic of science, the outer shell of knowledge; it is a superfluous addition to what is essential, worthwhile, and useful. The higher culture climbs, the more immeasurably the realm of distinct knowledge, the actual realm of representation spreads. The *twilight* shrinks ever smaller before the intruding light. Now the clear midday of enlightenment is at hand. Poetry—such charming child-ishness is no longer appropriate for[64] the last decade of our philosophical century. It is about time that we stop this." [119M]

Thus did a particular component of fine art, a fleeting condition of an earlier stage of its culturation [*Bildung*], become confused with its essence. As long as human nature exists, the drive to representation will be astir, and the advancement of beauty will endure. The necessary disposition of man, which must produce fine art as soon as it is able to evolve freely, is *eternal.* Art is an utterly peculiar activity of the human mind; it is distinguished from every other activity by *eternal boundaries.* All of human activity and suffering is a reciprocal effect of mind and nature. Either nature or the mind must be the ultimate basis for the existence of a particular communal product or the first determining impetus to its creation. In the first case, the result is *knowledge.* The character of the raw material determines the character of the diversity comprehended; it induces the mind to combine this diversity into a determined unity, and to continue the integration in a determined direction, to augment it to complete- [267] ness. Knowledge is an effect of nature in the mind. In the second case, however, the self-sufficient faculty must give itself a determined direction, and the character of the chosen unity determines the character of the diversity to be chosen, and that is chosen, ordered, and, if possible, formed in accordance with this purpose. The product is a *work of art* and an effect of the mind in nature. To the representational arts belong that realization of an eternal human objec- tive in the material of an external nature that is only mediately bound to man. This material will never extinguish; the eternal objectives will never stop being the objective of man. Beauty is no less separated by eternal boundaries from all other aspects of the vocation of humanity. Pure humanity—by this I under- stand the complete determination of the human race—is simply one and the same; it permits no subdivision. In its application to reality, however, pure humanity divides itself in various directions according to the eternal discre- pancy between the original faculties and circumstances, and according to the specific organs that these require. If I may be allowed to assume that the *faculty of sensibility* is specifically distinct from the faculty of imagination as well as the faculty of desire and that an intermediate state between the constraint of the law and need, namely, a condition of *free play* and an undetermined deter- minableness [*bestimmungslosen Bestimmbarkeit*] within human nature is just as necessary as the condition of obedient work and limited determinedness [*Bes-* [120M] *timmtheit*]: then beauty may be said to be of this ilk and *specifically distinct* from its kind—namely, from all of humanity as well as its secondary forms, from the other original components of the purpose of humanity.

But not only the aptitude for art and the dictates of beauty are physically and morally necessary; the *organs* of fine art also promise permanence. It [268] certainly does not have to be demonstrated that man will always have to deal with external *appearances?* The appearance of weakness, error, and need may indeed destroy the illumination that enlightenment provides: the *free* expression of the imagination at play cannot suffer under this. Yet one must not attribute the general advancement of representation and expression to a special type of *figurativeness,* or confuse the violent outbreak of the prolific passions of the wild men of nature with the essence of poetry.[65] In any case, it is very natural and understandable that, at a certain *midpoint* of artificial culturation [*Bildung*], brooding and pedantry lame and stifle that graceful play of the imagination and that refinement and coddling wear down and weaken the feelings. Constrained by an art that is incomplete, the strength of the drive is dulled; its liveliness is fettered; its ordinary movement is dissipated and confused. Sensibility and spirituality are so bound up with one another in man that their evolution can diverge in fugacious phases—but only within these phases. *On the whole,* they will keep step with one another; the part passed over will sooner or later make up what it missed. In fact, it seems that, with the growing magnitude of true spiritual development [*Geistesbildung*], man, rather than losing strength and sensitivity of feeling and hence *genuine aesthetic life force* (passion and grace), gains it.

It seems incomprehensible how men could convince themselves that Italian and French poetry, or even English and German poetry, have already had their *Golden Ages.* One misuses this term to such an extent that royal patronage, some famous names, a certain eagerness on the part of the public, and at the most, a high level of achievement in some trivial area seem sufficient to claim this title. Unfortunately, there was nothing left over for the ill-fated [269] Silver, Iron, and Lead Ages other than the sad fate of striving vainly with might and main after those eternal models. How can there even be a question of *perfect style,* when there is actually *no style at all* but only mannerism? In the strict sense of the word, not a single modern work of art—to say nothing of an [121M] entire age of poetry—has attained the summit of aesthetic *perfection.* The tacit presupposition that lies behind this: that it is the destiny of aesthetic development [*Bildung*] to arise like a plant or an animal, to gradually evolve, and then mature—yet only to deteriorate and finally to perish. Thus it always returns back to where its path first originated in an eternal cycle: this presupposition rests upon a simple misunderstanding, whose deep-seated source we will come across in what follows.

In the evolution of such a colossal and artificially organized mass like the peoples of Europe, a partial standstill or an occasional, apparent regression of culturation [*Bildung*] should not appear unusual. Yet even where one believes with certainty that the catastrophe has come to an end and aesthetic vitality is extinguished forever, one finds that the drama is far from over. Rather, this vitality lurks like a fire aglow under ashes and waits only for the opportune moment to flare up into a clear flame. It is truly wonderful how in our age the demand for the objective is everywhere astir, how the belief in the beautiful is being awakened, and unequivocal symptoms announce a more refined taste. The moment indeed seems ripe for an *aesthetic revolution,* by means of which the objective could become dominant in the aesthetic development [*Bildung*] of the moderns. Granted, nothing great occurs of its own accord without strength and resolve! It would be a self-defeating error if we were to lay our [270] hands in our laps and allow ourselves to be convinced that the taste of the age no longer required thorough improvement. As long as the objective is not predominant everywhere, this need is self-evident. The rule of the interesting, characteristic, and mannered presents a true *aesthetic heteronomy* within the poetic arts.[66] Just as all the elements of fine art are present in the chaotic anarchy evident throughout the entirety of modern poetry, so are all the types of aesthetic corruption—even those mutually opposed to one another— present. There is crudity next to affectation, enfeebled exiguity next to lawless wantonness. I have already explicitly declared that the claim of complete impotence, of hopeless degeneration, is false; I have acknowledged the magnitude of the aesthetic development [*Bildung*], the strength of the aesthetic vitality, of our age. Only the proper direction, the correct tone is missing. Only by means of these and together with these will every particular excellent aspect—which can be very harmful when not in its true context—maintain its true value and its proper meaning. For this, a complete transformation,[67] the total reversal of a revolution is necessary. [122M]

Aesthetic development [*Bildung*], in point of fact, has a divided nature. Either it is the *progressive evolution of a skill*—as such, it enlarges, sharpens, refines; indeed, it enlivens, strengthens, and elevates the original disposition. Or it is an absolute *legislation* that organizes force—it resolves the strife of particular beautiful elements, and promotes the agreement of all according to [271] the needs of the whole; it dictates strict correctness, elegant proportions, and completeness; it forbids the confusion of original aesthetic boundaries, and banishes the mannered as well as every aesthetic heteronomy. In a word: it achieves *objectivity.*

The aesthetic revolution[68] presupposes two necessary postulates as pre- liminary conditions of its possibility. The first of these is *aesthetic vitality.* Neither the genius of the artist alone, nor the primordial force of ideal representation and aesthetic energy allow themselves either to be acquired or supplanted. There is also an original, natural gift of the genuine *expert*, which, if it is already present, can frequently be cultivated [*gebildet*]; if it is lacking, however, no amount of cultivation [*Bildung*] can replace it. One cannot learn or teach perspicuous vision, discriminating sense, or that enhanced imaginative receptivity. But even the most felicitous disposition is inadequate to make a great artist or a great expert. Without the strength and scope of the ethical faculty, without harmony of mind—or at the least a general inclination toward it—no one will reach the all-holy penetralia of the temple of the muses. Hence the second necessary postulate for the individual artist and expert as well as[69] the public as a whole—*morality*. Correct taste, one could say, is the *developed* feeling of an ethically noble mind. It is impossible, moreover, that the taste of

[272] an immoral man could be correct and in harmony with itself. The Stoics in this regard justly claimed that only a wise man could be a perfect writer and expert. Certainly man has the capability—simply by means of freedom—to direct and organize the manifold forces of his mind. He is also able to impart a better direction and a proper tone to his aesthetic ability. Yet he has to *want* to; he has to have the force to want it, and the self-sufficiency to persevere in the resolution. No one can impart these to him if he does not find them in himself.

Admittedly, goodwill alone is not adequate, just as a bare foundation does not ensure the construction of a building. Vitality that is decadent and not at harmony with itself requires critique and censorship. And this presupposes

[123M] *legislation*. A perfect aesthetic legislation would be the first *organ* of an aesthetic revolution.[70] Its mission would be to guide brute vitality, to resolve what is in struggle into equilibrium, to organize the lawless into harmony; to impart a secure foundation, a certain direction, and a legitimate mood to aesthetic development [*Bildung*]. We do not need to look long for the *legislative power* of the aesthetic development [*Bildung*] of the moderns. It is already established. It is theory: for understanding was from the beginning the guiding principle of culturation [*Bildung*]. *Incorrect* concepts have long dominated art and misguided it into detours; *correct* concepts must lead it back to the proper path. In the modern age, artists as well as the public have always expected and demanded *correction* and satisfactory laws from theory. A *complete* aesthetic theory would not only be a reliable guide for culturation [*Bildung*], but it would also—by destroying harmful prejudices—unleash *vitality* and clear its path of

[273] obstacles. The laws of aesthetic theory have only true authority in as much as they are acknowledged and sanctioned by the major portion of public opinion. If the need for a universal truth indeed characterizes the age, then a reputation attained by disreputable means, such as the rhetorical arts, will be of brief duration. For one-sided untruths destroy themselves and outdated prejudices

fall apart on their own accord. In perfect and free agreement with itself, theory can then provide its laws the most well-grounded reputation, and elevate itself to a true *public force*. Only by means of *objectivity* can it live up to its mission.

Let us assume though that there were an objective aesthetic theory—which is more than we could boast of up until now. *Pure* science only determines the organization of the experience, the pigeonholes for the contents of intuition. By itself it would be *empty*—just as experience would be confused, without sense or purpose—and it is only in connection with a *perfect history* that it would be able to truly impart lessons about the nature of art and its genres. Science needs the experience of an art that would be a completely perfect example of its type, art *kat' exochen*, whose exceptional history would be the *general natural history of art*. Moreover, the thinker does not come innocent and unscathed to scientific scrutiny. He is infected by the influence of experiences that are distorted; he brings prejudices—which could impart an entirely false orientation to his investigation—even into the domain of pure abstraction. Even with the most sincere avidity it is not in his power to renounce these powerful prejudices at one fell stroke: for he would have to have already grasped truth in its purity in order to see the abyss of error, and to realize how wrong the procedure of his method is.[71] For a twofold reason, therefore, it requires a *perfect intuition*. Partly in order to provide an example and instance of his conception; partly in order to provide the facts and documentation of his inquiry. [274/124M]

Yet the gap between theory and praxis, between the law and particular deed, is infinitely great. It would be all too easy if the artist would be capable of producing the utmost beauty in his works by means of the simple concepts of a proper taste and a perfect style. The law must become *inclination*. Life only comes from life; vitality generates vitality. The law as such is empty. In order that it be *fulfilled* and its actual application be possible, it requires an intuition within which it visibly appears in harmonious completeness—that is, an ultimate *aesthetic prototype*.

Even the term "imitation" is insulting and is denounced by all those who imagine themselves to be born geniuses. Understood by this term is, in fact, the violence that a strong and great nature exerts on the powerless. But I know of no other word than *imitation* to describe the action of those—be they artist or expert—who appropriate to themselves the legitimacy of that prototype, without allowing themselves to be restricted by the peculiarity that the outward form, the husk of the universal spirit, may still yet carry with it. It is self-evident that this imitation is utterly impossible to achieve without the greatest autonomy. I speak here of that *disclosure of the beautiful* by means of which the expert comes into contact with the artist, and by means of which the artist comes into [275] contact with the divine. This is much like the magnet that does not just attract iron but, rather, imparts a magnetic force through contact.

Does the divine appear in earthly form? Can the limited ever be whole, the finite complete, the particular universal? Is there among men an art that deserves to be called art as such? Are there mortal works in which the law of eternity is visible?

With judicial majesty the muse surveys the book of ages, the assembly of peoples. Everywhere her strict gaze finds only the constant alternation of crudity and affectation, shabbiness and excess. Rarely does a gentle smile at the charming playfulness of childlike innocence brighten her indignant solemnity.

Only in the case of one people did fine art correspond to the great dignity of its destiny.

[125M]   Only in the case of the *Greeks* was art equally free from the constraints of necessity and the rule of the understanding. Beautiful plays were sacred to the Greeks—from the first beginnings of Greek culture [*Bildung*] up until the last moment while still a breath of genuine Greek sensibility lived.[72]

This *holiness of beautiful plays* and this *freedom of the representational arts* are the actual *characteristics of genuine Greekness. For all barbarians, however, beauty in itself is not good enough.* Lacking a sense for the unconditioned purposefulness of its purposeless play, they required assistance and advice from outside sources. With uncouth as well as sophisticated non-Greeks, art is simply a slave of either sensibility or reason. Only by means of a remarkable, rich, new, and unusual content, only by means of voluptuous material can

[276][74]   representation become important and interesting to them.[73]

Already during the initial stage of culturation [*Bildung*] and while still under the tutelage of nature, *Greek poetry* encompasses the whole of human nature in uniform completion, in the most felicitous equilibrium and without a biased disposition or a pronounced eccentricity. Its vigorous growth soon evolves into self-sufficiency and reaches the point where the mind attains a decided predominance in its struggle with nature; and its golden age reaches the highest peak of ideality (the complete self-determination of art) and beauty that is possible in natural culturation [*Bildung*] of any sort. What is peculiar to it is that it is the most strong, pure, most specific, simple, and complete copy of human nature in general. The history of the Greek poetic arts is a general, natural history of the poetic arts, a perfect and legislative intuition.

In Greece beauty grew without supervision of an artificial kind; it essentially grew wild. Under this propitious heaven representational art was not a learned accomplishment; rather, it was *primordial nature.* Its development [*Bildung*] was nothing else but the *freest evolution of the most felicitous disposition.* Greek poetry found its beginning in the rawest simplicity: but this meager origin does not discredit it. Its most basic character is simple and unostentatious; it is unspoiled. Here you will find neither an insipid reverie, nor a distorted imitation of a foreign national character, nor an eccentric and well-entrenched one-sidedness. Here the arbitrariness of inappropriate concepts could not restrict the free growth of nature, or rend or destroy its harmony, or falsify its simplicity, or distort the course and direction of culturation [*Bildung*]. Greek poetry distinguishes itself early on by means of a certain something from all other national poetries at a similar stage of the childhood of culture. Greek poetry is equally removed from Oriental bombast and Nordic melancholy; it is full of vigor but without harshness, full of grace but without weakness. It is thereby anomalous[75] in that it, more than any other poetry, is purely human and true to the universal law out of its own inclination. Already in its childhood its higher calling announces itself—namely, to represent not the coincidental but, rather, the essential and necessary, to strive not after the particular but the general. It also had its *mythic origin,* like every free evolution of the poetic faculty. During the initial period of its evolution, Greek poetry moved back and forth between fine art and legend. It was an uncertain mixture of tradition and invention, of figurative doctrine, history, and free play. But what a legend it was. Never was there a more ingenious or ethical legend. *Greek myth*—like the truest reflection in the clearest mirror—is the most precise and exquisite figurative language for all eternal wishes of the mind of man in all its wonderful and necessary contradictions; it is a small, complete world of the most beautiful presentiments of the childlike poeticizing reason. Poetry, song, dance, and sociability—*festive joy* was the sweet bond of community that joined men and Gods. And, indeed, the meaning of their legends, customs—especially their festivals as well as the object of their worship—was the genuine divinity: the *most pure humanity.* In delightful images the Greeks[76] worshiped liberal abundance, autonomous force, and law-governed harmony.

[277]

[126M]

[278]

By means of a—for its kind—unique combination of the most felicitous circumstances nature did something really *radical* in its preferential treatment of these fondlings. Often human development [*Bildung*]—immediately after its initial impetus, and while it is still too weak to withstand the hard struggle with fate without any further careful nurturing—is abandoned to its own weaknesses and every unfavorable coincidence. A people can indeed boast of good fortune if, simply by means of the propitiousness of its situation, it can arrive with effort at an significant stage of a *one-sided* culturation [*Bildung*]. In the case of the Greeks, the initial stage of culturation [*Bildung*] already unified and encompassed entirely that which is usually only present as divided and separate at the highest stage of culture. Just as in the mind of Homer's Diomedes all forces are uniformly—and in the most beautiful accord—harmonized into a perfect equilibrium: so here humanity develops uniformly and completely. Already in the heroic age of mythic art, Greek nature poetry

unified the most beautiful blossomings of the most noble Nordic nature poetry
and the most exquisite southern nature poetry. It is the most perfect poetry of
its kind.

[127M]　　Many like *Homer.* Only a few, however, fully comprehend his beauty.
Just as many travelers search great distances for what they could just as easily
find at home and that would be of just as good quality and closer at hand: so
people often admire in Homer only that which is similar to what can be found
in any Nordic or southern barbarian—so long as he is a great poet. That which
makes Homer unique is seldom noticed; it is usually not considered at all.
Exact truth, primordial force, simple grace, charming naturalness are qualities
that the Greek bard probably shares with just about any of his Indian or Celtic
[279]　brothers. There are, however, other characteristic traits of Homeric poetry, that
are unique to the *Greek poet.*

　　One such Greek trait is the *completeness* of Homer's view of the whole of
human nature, which—by virtue of the most felicitous *symmetry* and most
perfect *equilibrium*—is far removed from the one-sided limitation of an eccentric disposition, from the distortion of artificial misculturation [*Mißbildung*].
The *range* of his poetry is as unlimited as the scope of human nature itself. The
most extreme ends of the most diverse tendencies—whose original seeds lay
hidden already in the general nature of humanity—genially join together with
one another, as in uninhibited, childlike play. His serene and pure representation unifies fantastic strength with inner peace, and the most clear-cut specificity with the most exquisite subtlety of outline.

　　In the morals of his heroes vitality and grace are in equilibrium. They are
strong but not uncouth, gentle without being soft, intelligent without being
indifferent. Although *Achilles* is more frightful than a fighting lion when angry,
he is acquainted nonetheless with the tears of tender pain on the faithful breast
of a loving mother; he assuages his loneliness with the gentle passion of sweet
songs. With a heartfelt sigh he looks back at his own mistakes, at the great harm
that the stubborn presumption of a proud king and the rash anger of a young
hero have caused. With a charming wistfulness he consecrates locks of hair on
the grave of his beloved friend.[77] In the arms of an honorable elder—the father
of his hated enemy made unfortunate by him—he can melt into tears of
compassion.[78] The general outline of a character like Achilles could have
perhaps also occurred in the imagination of a northern or southern Homer: yet
these finer traits of composition were only possible for the Greek. Only the
Greek could unify and blend together the volatile temper, the teeming celerity
of a young lion with so much spirit, morality, and soul. Even in battles, at the
moment where he is so filled with rage that he—unmoved by the pleading of
his opponent—runs through the breast of his vanquished enemy, he remains
human, indeed even charming, and appeases us by means of a wonderfully

moving meditation.[79] The character of *Diomedes,* however, is already in its   [280/128M]
original composition entirely Greek.[80] In his serene grandeur, his unassuming
accomplishment, the peaceful spirit of the poet mirrors itself most clearly and
purely.[81]

A *sovereign humanity* separates the Homeric heroes as well as the poet
himself from all non-Greek heroes and bards. In portraying every specific
situation, in each type of mental disposition, the poet strives, in as much as the
context allows, for the *ethical beauty* of which this childlike age's uncorrupted
sensuousness is capable. Ethical strength and abundance predominate in
Homer's poetry; ethical unity and steadfastness are, where they occur, not a
spontaneous work of the mind but, rather, a felicitous product of a formative
[*bildende*] nature. But tremendous strength and sensual pleasure alone do not
arouse and grip his mind. Not the least of the exceptional qualities of the Greek
poet are the unassuming charm of quiet *domesticity* (especially in the *Odyssey*);
the beginnings of a *bourgeois sensibility;* and the first stirrings of a *refined
sociability.*

Just compare this to the spiritless monotony of barbaric chivalry![82] In the
modern knight of Romantic poetry heroism is distorted by the most bizarre
concepts into the strangest forms and trends so that there are few traces left of
the original magic of the independent life of the hero. Instead of morals and
feelings one finds here barren concepts and dull prejudices; instead of liberal
abundance a muddled exiguity; instead of active vitality a lifeless mass.   [281]
Compare them with those representations[83] in which just the smallest atom of
a *nobler life* glows; compare these with the Homeric heroes, whose composition
[*Bildung*] is so *genuinely human*[84]—as only the composition [*Bildung*] of a
hero can be. In their minds the active whole is not divided but, rather, thoroughly interrelated: ideas and undertakings are here intimately melted into one
another; all parts are in complete agreement with one another, and the rich
abundance of primordial vigor gracefully organizes itself into a satisfying
whole.

One often terms this "indulgence"—pampering the senses and thereby
profaning the dignity of humanity so that one recognizes no purpose of art
other than that which cajoles animality. There is, however, another feature
bearing the same name, which shies away from doing injury to the mind:
ethical indulgence. In non-Greek poetries our feelings are often affronted by a
certain something even there where the spirit has been refined to the utmost
degree, even there where the most delicate blossomings of the most delicate
sensibility are the freshest. There is actually no barbaric work that is entirely   [129M]
free of everything that would incense an authentic Greek sensibility. These
people do not seem to suspect that *displeasure* immediately destroys the enjoyment of the beautiful; that *needless baseness* is the greatest mistake of which a

poet can be guilty. One would reprimand musicians who, for no reason, conclude with an unresolved dissonance; yet one forgives or admires the poet, who, lacking all feeling for the harmony of the whole, injures the delicate ear of the mind by means of the most flagrant discord. With Homer, however, every wicked deed is *prepared* and *resolved.* Through a moment of youthful arrogance Patrocles resolves us with his death, and what would otherwise be bitter displeasure, becomes thus gentle compassion. The arrogance of Hector is a [282]   preparation for his downfall. If the excessive wrath of Achilles had not tempted him to moments of frenzy and injustice, his indignation, the loss of his friend, his pain, the unalterable brevity of his glorious life would do deep injury to us and fill us with bitterness. The quiet power, the wise serenity of Diomedes corresponds to the unadulterated and always untroubled purity of his good fortune and his unenvied fame. Just as the father of the gods thoughtfully weighs the fate of warriors on the scales of judgment, so does Homer, with artistic wisdom, allow his heroes to founder and ascend, not according to whim and coincidence, but according to the sacred decisions of humanity at its purest.

One should not think that that which is worthy of imitation in Greek poetry is the privilege of a few chosen geniuses—as is the case with every instance of splendid originality among the moderns. The merely individual would, accordingly, not be worthy of imitation; nor would it be possible to appropriate it entirely: for only the *universal* is the law and prototype for all ages and peoples. Greek beauty was the common property of a public taste, *the spirit of the whole.* Even those poems that reveal little artistic wisdom and meager inventiveness are conceived, outlined, and executed in the same spirit, the traits of which we read more definitely and clearly in Homer and other writers of the first order. By means of the same traits they distinguish themselves from all non-Greek poems as the best *poems.*

Greek poetry has its idiosyncrasies, which are often eccentric enough: for even though Greek culture [*Bildung*] is purely human, the external form can be very idiosyncratic; it is probably all the more so because the spirit is so true to [130M]   the universally valid law. Most of these *aesthetic paradoxes* are only apparent; in [283]   fact, they contain great significance. Such is the case with the satyric drama, the dithyramb, the lyric chorus of the Dorians, and the dramatic chorus of the Athenians. Only out of complete ignorance of the actual nature of art and its types did one consider such traits as merely individual and content oneself with a historical genesis of it. The facts, moreover, were available only in rough outline. As long as one does not know the necessary formative laws [*Bildungsgesetze*] of art, one will feel one's way in the dark in the history of art, and will have no guiding thread to deduce from the known to the unknown. If one were only to analyze thoroughly the character of these anomalies according to sound principles and concepts one would be surprised at the result of such a *philosophical deduction,*[85] and one would come again upon the thorough objectivity of Greek poetry. Even in an age where all of Greek poetry divided itself into many clearly distinct styles—like so many branches of a common trunk— and its compass thereby became limited to the same extent that its vitality was enhanced: even in the lyric genre, whose actual object is *beautiful peculiarity,* Greek poetry preserves nonetheless its constant tendency toward the objective by means of the type and spirit of representation, which—in as much as the particular limits of its peculiar style and its subject matter allow— approximates the purely human, elevates the individual to the general, and represents in the peculiar actually only the universal.

Greek poetry decayed to an incredible extant and ultimately became utterly decadent. But *even in the most extreme degeneracy* there remain traces of that which make it universal—up until the point it no longer has a distinct [284] character. To such an extent *Greekness* is nothing else than a nobler, purer humanity! In the era of the learned poetic arts there were neither public morals, nor public taste. The poems of the *Alexandrians* are without any actual morals, without spirit and life; they are indifferent, dead, paltry, and clumsy. Instead of a perfect organization and a living, unified whole, these pathetic efforts are just patched together out of sundered fragments. They contain only a few beautiful traits, yet no complete and whole beauty. Nonetheless, its painstaking representation contains—in its thoroughly fine specificity, its complete freedom from all the impure admixture of subjectivity and the technical mistakes resulting from monstrous combinations and poetic falsehood—an *extreme natural perfection of its* admittedly reproachable nature, a *certain classical something,* which is not dissimilar to what scholars of the Greek plastic arts notice in the [131M] remnants of the pictorial arts of even the worst era, or from the hand of the most average artist. Bombastic, overladen ornament belongs to the general bad taste of the age. Mistakes in execution can be attributed to amateurs. It is solely the *spirit* in which the work was conceived, outlined, and formed [*ausgebildet*] that contains at least traces of the perfect ideal that is a valid law and general prototype for all ages and peoples. Thus one can find in *Apollonius* very often truly classical details, and every now and then one comes upon reminders of the [285] former divinity of the Greek poetic arts.[86] Such traits are to be found in the modesty of the heroic Jason and his meditative serenity during the heroic band's great expedition as well as during the loss of Hercules; the splendid description of Telamon, Hercules, Aeëtes, and Idmon; the delightful play of Eros and Ganymede; the grace that is evident in the entire episode of Hypsipyle and Medea. The more precise specificity, the finer delicacy, the thorough workmanship of his painstaking work—traits that he has more of than the most learned of all Roman poets—are so many left-over traces of genuine Greek culture [*Bildung*].

Fate shaped [*bildete*] the Greek not only into the utmost that a son of nature can be, but it also only withdrew its motherly care when Greek culture [*Bildung*] was independent and mature and did not require any more external assistance and guidance. With this decisive step—by means of which freedom acquired predominance over nature—man entered into an entirely new order of things; man began a new stage of its evolution. Man determines, directs, and organizes his vitality himself, shapes [*bildet*] his abilities according to the inner laws of his mind. The beauty of art is not merely the gift of a generous nature; rather, it is his own handiwork, the property of his mind. The spiritual achieves predominance over the sensual. He determines independently the direction of his taste, and orders representation. He dedicates himself not simply to what is present at hand but he also independently brings forth the beautiful. And when the initial venture into maturity limits the compass of art by means of a precisely determined style, this loss is replaced by the inward power and sovereignty of the concentrated vitality. The epic age of Greek poetry can still nonetheless be compared to those of other national poetries. In the age of the [286]   lyric they stand alone. Only Greek poetry attained *in its entirety* that stage of culture [*Bildung*] characterized by *autonomy;* only in it was ideal beauty *public.* As plentiful and marvelous as the examples may be in modern poetry, they are [132M]   just individual exceptions. The bulk remains far behind this stage and, in fact, falsifies these exceptions. With the predominant disbelief in a more divine beauty, that which remains unappreciated loses its natural confidence, and the struggle that should make it accepted profanes it no less than the inhospitable pride that must take the place of the pleasure of discovery. From the earliest times there have been nations that have surpassed the Greeks in skill; they have not thereby understood the greatness of the actual culture [*Bildung*] of the Greeks. But skills are only the necessary adjuncts of culture [*Bildung*], the implements of freedom. Only the evolution of a pure humanity constitutes *true culturation* [*Bildung*]. Where did free humanity achieve such a thorough predominance in the entirety of a people as with the Greeks? Where was culture [*Bildung*] so genuine, and genuine culture [*Bildung*] so public? In fact, there is hardly a more sublime spectacle in the course of human history as that great moment in which—suddenly and essentially of its own accord, and by means of the simple evolution of the inner life force—there emerges republicanism in the Greek states, enthusiasm and wisdom in ethics, logical and systematic coherence (instead of the mythic organization of the imagination) in the sciences, and the *ideal* in the Greek arts.

If freedom has predominance over nature, culturation [*Bildung*] that is unhampered and left to itself must move forward in the direction selected, and climb ever higher until its course is impeded by an external force or until, by means of sheer inner evolution, the relation between freedom and nature alters itself all over again. If the *entire* composite human drive is not simply the motive but also the *guiding principle of culturation* [*Bildung*], if the culturation [*Bildung*] is *natural* and not artificial, if the original disposition is the most felicitous, and if the external sustenance is perfect: then all components of the striving force of a humanity that is forming itself evolve, grow, and come *uniformly* to completion until evolution has reached the point when no more fullness can be achieved without dividing and destroying the *harmony of the whole.* [287]

The utmost that fine art can attain by means of the most unfettered evolution of the most felicitous disposition will be achieved if the ultimate level of the development [*Bildung*] of the most perfect genre of the most splendid art meets felicitously with an auspicious moment in the tide of public taste, if a great artist earns the favor of fate, and knows how to fill out in a worthy manner the vague outlines that necessity sketches.

Greek poetry truly attained this *ultimate limit of the natural culturation* [*Bildung*] of art and taste, this *utmost pinnacle of free beauty.* Culturation [*Bildung*] has attained a state of *perfection* if the inner striving force has fully unfolded itself, if the intention has been completely achieved, and no expectation remains unfulfilled in the uniform completeness of the whole. This state is termed a *golden age* when an entire complex of concurrently existing elements obtains. The pleasure that the works of the golden age of Greek art affords could indeed be further augmented, but it nonetheless harbors no disorder or deficiency—it is *complete and self-sufficient.* For this level of accomplishment, I know of no more appropriate name than *ultimate beauty.* Not simply a beauty about which nothing more beautiful could be thought but, rather, the complete example of the unattainable idea that essentially becomes here utterly apparent: *the prototype of art and taste.* [133M]

[288]

The sole measure according to which we could appreciate the highest pinnacle of Greek poetry is provided by the *limits of all art.* "But why," it will be asked, "is art not capable of endless perfection? Are there limits to its progressive development [*Bildung*]?"

Art is infinitely perfectible. An absolute maximum in its continuous evolution is not possible: yet a conditioned, *relative*[87] *maximum,* an unsurpassable, *fixed approximation* is possible. The mission of art consists, namely, of two entirely distinct components: it consists, in part, of specific *laws* that can either be followed entirely or disregarded entirely; and, in part, of insatiable, vague *demands,* within which even the greatest excess allows itself to be augmented. Every force that is genuinely present is capable of enhancement and every finite, real perfection is capable of an infinite growth. When it comes to *proportions,* however, there can be no more or less; the law-governedness of an object can neither be increased nor decreased. Thus all actual elements of fine art are individually capable of infinite growth; but when it comes to the integration of these different elements there are absolute laws concerning reciprocal relations.

   Beauty in the broadest sense (in which it encompasses the sublime, beauty in the strict sense, and the charming) is the *pleasurable manifestation of the good.*[88] There appears to be established for every individual temper a fixed limit, which neither pain nor joy can exceed if all equanimity is not to come to an end and concomitantly the aim of passion and desire not to be forsaken. In general, however—and without any special effort—something greater can be thought beyond every existing measure of energy. By *energy* I understand everything that sensually awakens and stimulates the composite drive in order to provide it the pleasure of the purely spiritual; the motive force might be either pain or joy. Energy, however, is only the means and organ of ideal art; it is essentially the *physical life force* of pure beauty, which gives rise to and supports the sensual appearance of the spiritual, just as the mind that is free can only exist empirically in the element of an animalistic organization. In the same way there is for each particular receptivity a *specific sphere of perceptibility*—if I may put it this way—-in between a too great proximity and a too great distance. In and of itself the appearance of the spiritual can always become more lively, specific, and distinct. Although it is never able to reach its goal, it is capable of endless perfection as long as it remains on the level of appearance: for otherwise the general, which should appear in the particular, would have to transform itself into the particular. This is impossible because both are separated by an endless chasm. However, the imitation of the actual can be perfected endlessly: for the abundance of each particular is inexhaustible, and no reproduction can ever change over into its prototype. I can presuppose as self-evident that the *good*—or that which simply should be (as the pure object of the free drive); that the pure I (not as theoretical faculty, but as a practical law); that the genre whose forms are knowledge, ethics, and beauty; that the whole, whose elements are multiplicity, unity, and totality can be present within reality in only a limited way:[89] for man, who is himself pieced together, can in this heterogeneous life approximate his pure nature only in the infinite, without ever entirely reaching it.

   All these elements of the beautiful—charm, outward appearance, goodness—are capable of endless perfection. However, immutable laws obtain for the reciprocal relations of these elements. The sensuous should only be the

[289]
[134M]

[290]

medium of beauty, not the goal of art. If an unspoilt sensuousness predominates in an early stage of culturation [*Bildung*], *abundance* becomes the goal of the writer. Self-sufficiency should not be met with the reproach that it has to evolve gradually and that it can only attain autonomous self-determination under the tutelage of nature. Homer's sensuousness does not result in a transgression of the law; rather, the law does not yet actually exist. If art has been law-governed, and ceases to be so any longer, abundance rules again but in an entirely different manner. It is no longer pure sensuousness but rather lavish excess, *anarchic indulgence.* Those three elements of beauty—multiplicity, unity, and totality—are nothing other than so many ways in which man in his purity can attain actual existence in the world; they are different points of contact between the mind and nature. Individually considered, all three have the same worth; one, like the other, has the same unconditioned, infinite value. *Even abundance is holy,* and may, in the unification of all elements, obey in no other manner than *freely* the law of its organization: for *multiplicity* is already the first form of life—and not raw matter, with which it is often confused. *Isonomy* should not be sublated by order; indeed, the *law of the relation of the unified elements of beauty* is immutably determined. Not multiplicity but totality should be the first determining ground and the ultimate goal of every perfect form of beauty. Mind should prevail over content and passion. Spirit should prevail over what is alluring and not be *used* in order to rouse life and stimulate the senses. One could achieve such a goal at much less cost! Style represents the enduring relations of the original and essential components of beauty or taste. One could attribute a *perfect style* to those works of art and those ages that entirely and willingly obey the requisite law in these relations.

[135M]

[291]

Other than this absolute, aesthetic law for every taste, there are also two absolute *technical* laws for all the representational arts. The elements of representational art, which combine the possible with the actual, are the incarnation of the general and the imitation of the individual. There are no limits, as has been remarked, in the perfection of both components: for their interrelation, however, an immutable law is absolutely necessary. The goal of fine, representational art is the unconditioned; the particular may not itself be an aim (subjectivity). If this is not the case, fine art sinks to the level of an imitative dexterity, which serves a physical need or a particular purpose of the understanding. Yet the means are entirely necessary and it must at least seem to serve freely. *Objectivity* is the most appropriate term for this law-governed interrelation of the general and the particular in a free representation. Moreover, every individual work of art is in no way chained to the law of actuality but is definitely limited by the *laws of inner possibility.* It may not contradict itself; it must be in complete agreement with itself. This *technical accuracy*—as I would rather term it instead of "truth"[90] because this word evokes the laws of actuality to too great

[292/136M]

an extent and is so often abused by slavishly imitative artists who only imitate the particular—may not, in cases where it occasions conflict, dominate beauty itself, but it may restrict it: for it is the condition of possibility of a work of art. Without inner accord a representation would not only sublate itself, but it would also not be able to attain its end (beauty). Only when the whole of beauty in its completion has been divided and broken up, and excessive abundance dominates taste, will the regularity of proportion as well as the symmetry of this abundance be sacrificed.

It does not require much renunciation for frailty not to indulge in excess; and where vigor is lacking, law-governedness is no particular achievement. A poem of perfect style and faultless accuracy but without spirit and life would amount only to an exiguity of no value. But even when a poem joins such perfect law-governedness with the utmost vigor that one can expect from a mortal artist, one can nonetheless still not hope to attain the ultimate goal, if its compass, instead of being incomplete, is rather limited by means of the precisely determined style of a certain—admittedly beautiful but nonetheless one-sided—peculiarity, as in that of the Doric lyric. The poet can lay no claim to perfection as long as he, like Aeschylus, raises more expectations than can be satisfied. Only that *work of art—which in the most perfect genre, and with the greatest strength and wisdom entirely fulfills the relevant aesthetic and technical laws, and which corresponds harmoniously with endless demands*—can be an unsurpassable example in which the whole purpose of fine art becomes as manifest as it can in an actual work of art.

[293]

Only where all elements of art and taste evolve, form, and complete themselves in equal proportion is the greatest beauty possible—that is, in *natural* culturation [*Bildung*]. In artificial culturation [*Bildung*] this *symmetry* is irrecoverably lost[91] by the arbitrary division and mixture undertaken by the regulative understanding. In particular instances of perfection and beauty, it can perhaps by far surpass unfettered evolution: but that greatest beauty is that which has become an *organically formed whole,* and which would be torn asunder by the smallest division, destroyed by the slightest excess. The artificial apparatus of the regulative understanding can appropriate to itself the law-governedness[92] to be found in the golden age of the art produced by formative [*bildenden*] nature, but it can never entirely reproduce its symmetry. The elementary whole never reorganizes itself once it is broken up. *The pinnacle of the natural culturation [Bildung] of fine art* remains thus for all times the *great prototype of artistic progress.*

[137M]

We are accustomed, for what reasons I don't know, to conceive of the *limits of poetry* too narrowly. If representation does not describe, like the poetic arts, but rather truly imitates or naturally expresses itself like the sensuous arts, then its freedom is more narrowly constrained because of the limits of the tools at hand and the specific materials. Should the scope of the material be very [294] limited, or the tool very simple, in a certain type of art, one could easily think that a favored people has attained a height that could never be surpassed. Perhaps the Greeks never actually attained these heights in the plastic arts. Painting and music already have a free rein—the instrument is more concentrated, more manifold and encompassing. It would be rash to want to set an outermost limit of perfection to it. How much less can such a limit be set for poetry, which is limited by no particular material in either compass or in strength? whose tool, an arbitrary sign-language,[93] is the work of man, and is endlessly perfectible and corruptible?—*Unrestricted compass* is the one great advantage of poetry, which it perhaps perforce needs in order to make up for the advantages the plastic arts have, namely, the thorough specificity of that which perseveres, and to make up for the advantage music has, namely, the thorough liveliness of the mutable. Both render intuition and sensation directly to the sensibility; to the mind they often speak only in an often obscure language and in a roundabout manner. They can only present thoughts and morals in an indirect fashion. By means of the imagination, the poetic arts speak in an often opaque and ambiguously vague but all-encompassing language directly to the spirit and heart. The advantage of those sensuous arts— infinite specificity and infinite liveliness, that is, *particularity*—is not so much a merit of art as the borrowed property of nature. They are hybrids that fall between pure nature and pure art. The single actual *pure art* without borrowed vitality and external assistance is poetry. [138M]

If one compares the different types of art with one another, one cannot speak of a greater or lesser value of the purpose. Otherwise, the entire investigation would be as nonsensical as the question: "Who was more virtuous, Socrates or Timoleon?"[94] For the infinite does not tolerate comparison; the enjoyment of the beautiful has unconditional value. But in the perfection of the different means of attaining such an end, there are stages, degrees of more or less. No art can embrace such a broad compass in one work as poetry. But none [295] has such means *to join together so much into a unity and to augment the joining into an unconditioned, complete whole.* The plastic arts, music, and the lyric are actually on the same level with regard to unity. They posit one extremely homogeneous diversity right next to or after one another and strive to develop the remaining diversity organically out of that which has been posited. *Character*, as that which endures in ideas and initiatives could only in God be simple, determined through itself, and completed in itself. In the realm of appearance its unity remains conditioned; it must still contain a diversity that cannot be determined through itself. A truly solitary appearance is completely determined and explained by the *interconnectedness of the entire world* to which it belongs. The same is the case with the fragment of a merely possible world. The dramatic character is determined completely by its position in the whole, and its part in the action. An action is only completed in time; thus the sculptor can present no complete action. Even if the plastic character is ever so determined, he necessarily posits the *world* in which it is actually at home—and which can never be presented as such—as already known. Even if this world is the Olympian world and the interpretation of it an easy matter: the most perfect statue is still only a sundered, incomplete fragment, not a whole perfect unto itself. The most that images can attain is an *analogon of unity*. The unity of the lyric artist and musician consists in the *similarity* of some sentiments, which have been lifted out of the entire range of interrelated states and which rule over the rest; and it consists in the complete *subordination* of these remaining

[296]   sentiments to those that dominate. The diversity and freedom that is necessary set narrow limits to the perfection of this interrelation—to say nothing of the *perfection of the integration*. *The perfection of the integration* is the second great advantage of poetry. Only the tragedian, whose particular goal is to join the

[139M]   greatest breadth and the strongest vigor with the greatest unity, can give his work a *perfect organization,* the beautiful structure of which is disturbed neither by the smallest lack, nor by the slightest superfluity. He alone can present a *complete action,* the sole unconditioned whole in the realm of appearance. An entirely accomplished act, a completely realized objective yields the fullest satisfaction. A completed poetic action is a whole unto itself, a *technical world.*[95]

The earlier types of Greek poetry are in part the quite imperfect experiments of a still immature culture [*Bildung*], much like the epic of the mythic age; they are also in part one-sided limited styles, which split up and divide evenly among themselves a complete beauty, much like the different schools of the age of lyric. The most splendid of the different types of Greek poetry are to be found in *Attic tragedy*. It determines, purifies, elevates, unifies, organizes into a new whole all the isolated elements of perfection to be found in the earlier types, ages, and schools.

With true creativity, Aeschylus invented tragedy, sketched its outline, defined its limits, its direction, and its goal. What the bold poet sketched out, *Sophocles* carried out. He developed what Aeschylus invented, smoothes out his harshness, augments his deficiencies, and brings tragedy to completion—he thereby attains the utmost end of Greek poetry. Fortunately, he coincided with

[297]   the greatest moment of public Attic taste. Yet he also knew how to earn the favor of fate. He shared with his age the advantage of a perfect taste, a perfect style: the manner, however, in which he assumed his role and lived up to his vocation is entirely specific to him. He does not yield to either Aeschylus or Aristophanes when it comes to genial vitality: in perfection and serenity he is

the equal of Homer and Pindar, and he surpasses all his predecessors and successors in grace.

The *technical accuracy* of his representation is perfect. The *eurhythmics,* the uniform integration of his precise and richly structured works is as *canonical* as the proportions of the famous Doryphoros of Polycleitos.[96] The mature and full-grown organization of each of them is carried out to a *completeness* that is disrupted neither by the slightest deficiency, nor by a superfluous touch. Everything evolves *necessarily* out of a unity and even the smallest part belongs unconditionally to the *great law of the whole.*

The moderation with which he renounces even the most beautiful outgrowth and with which he would have resisted even the most alluring temptation to do damage to the equilibrium of the whole is for *this* writer a proof of his richness. For his law-governedness is *free,* his accuracy is *graceful,* and the *richest abundance* organizes itself of its own accord to a perfect yet pleasing [140M] harmony. The unity of his dramas was not mechanically forced; rather, it *emerged organically.* Even the smallest side-branch enjoys its own life and appears simply to relegate itself freely to its place in the ordered context of the entire formation [*Bildung*]. With pleasure and without difficulty we follow the overwhelming torrent, we range over the spellbinding surface of his writing: for the *beauty* of a correct but simple and unconstrained *attitude* lends it an [298] unspeakable charm. The whole as well as the various parts are precisely differentiated and pleasingly grouped in the richest and simplest conglomerations. And struggle and calm, act and contemplation, humanity and fate obligingly alternate and freely unite throughout the action, as when one moment the solitary force erupts forth unrestrictedly, then the next moment two quickly alternating forces embrace one another in struggle, and then the next all individual elements are silent before the majestic mass of the chorus: thus even in the smallest speech one finds diversity gracefully multiplying itself and freely unifying itself.

Here there is not the slightest reminder of labor, art, and necessity. We are no longer aware of the medium; the shell vanishes, and we immediately enjoy pure beauty. This unpretentious perfection appears not to tarry by its own greatness or to care for its outward impression but only to be there for its own sake. These formations [*Bildungen*] appear not to have been made or to have become but, rather, to have been eternally present, or to have originated out of themselves, as the goddess of love arose effortlessly and at once perfect out of the ocean.

Equally blended together in the mind of Sophocles was the divine intoxication of Dionysus, the profound inventiveness of Athena, and the quiet level-headedness of Apollo.[97] With a magical ability his poetry transports spirits from their abodes into a higher world; with charming force he entices hearts and makes off with them. But as a great master in the rare art of what is *fitting*, he knows to win for himself *the greatest indulgence* by means of the most felicitous use of the greatest tragic force. He is forceful in what is full of passion as well as in what is full of dread; yet he is never bitter or shocking. Constant dread would paralyze us into unconsciousness; constant passion would overwhelm us. Sophocles, however, knows how to mix dread and passion beneficently into the most perfect equilibrium, how to season exquisitely with enchanting joy and cheerful grace in the appropriate places, and how to spread this beautiful vitality in equal measures over the whole.

[299]

His mastery of the *material*—as well as his felicitous selection from it, and his judicious use of the existing accounts[98]—is incredible. To always hit upon the best solution from so many, perhaps countless, possible solutions, to never stray beyond the delicate boundaries and to assert his complete freedom even within the most intricate parameters by skillfully submitting to necessity—this is the masterstroke of artistic wisdom. Even when a predecessor had anticipated the most fitting solution, he knew how to reappropriate the appropriated material. Despite coming to it after Aeschylus, he was able to be original in *Electra* without being unnatural.[99] Even in a play such as *Philoctetes*—the subject matter of which is rich in individual great portraits and felicitous insights but which remains on the whole inauspicious and incomplete—he knew how to shape it into a complete story, one that it is not lacking in graceful unity or in complete satisfaction.[100]

[141M]

The *Attic magic of his language* unifies the animated abundance of Homer and the delicate splendor of Pindar with a thoroughly developed specificity. The bold and noble but harsh, angular, and strident portraits of Aeschylus are refined, softened, and developed in the diction of Sophocles to a precise accuracy. The *perfection* of the Greek language was only possible in *Athens* where inventiveness, sociability, eloquence, and solicitude were essentially innate, where a comprehensive culture [*Bildung*] encompassed the limited advantages of Doric and Ionian culture [*Bildung*], where everything inward, in the context of restricted freedom and isonomy, could step forth into bold relief, and the most varied friction from the outside was whetted, burnished, and organized by means of the most animated struggle.

[300]

The *rhythm* of Sophocles unifies the vigorous flux, the teeming vitality, and the manly dignity of the Doric style with the rich abundance, the precipitate tenderness, and the delicate gracefulness of Ionian or Aeolian rhythms.

The *ideal of beauty*—which is predominant throughout all the works of Sophocles as well as in their individual features—is thoroughly perfected. The force of the individual essential components of beauty is symmetrical and the organization of the unified components thoroughly law-governed. *His style is perfect.* In each individual tragedy and in each individual case the degree of beauty is precisely determined by the limits of the material, the interrelation of the whole, and the nature of the particular situation.

The *ethical* beauty of all individual *dramatis personae* is only as great as these conditions allow. All actions and passions arise in as much as possible out of *morals* or character; and the particular characters, the specific morals, approximate, in as much as possible, pure humanity. The pointlessly bad is as unlikely to be found here as is futile pain; and the slightest impulse toward bitter indignation is strictly avoided.[101] [142M]

In contrast to the stories, there are as few incidents as possible—and these are all derived from *fate.* The incessant, necessary struggle between fate and humanity, however, is always resolved into harmony by means of another form of ethical beauty, until humanity finally—in as much as the laws of technical accuracy allow—achieves complete victory. *Contemplation*—this necessary internal echo of every great outward act or event—*sustains* and preserves the equilibrium of the whole. The quiet dignity of a beautiful ethos brings an order to the awful struggle and guides the bold, matchless energy—which forcibly breaks through every dam of order—back onto the gentle course of the eternal, steadfast law. In every instance, the conclusion of the entire work affords in the end the *fullest satisfaction:* for even if the outward appearance and prospect of humanity appears to decay, it triumphs nonetheless by means of inner conviction. The courageous resistance of the hero can in the end be defeated by the blind rage of fate: but the self-sufficient mind sustains itself nonetheless throughout all torments and ultimately vaults upward free, like the dying Hercules in *The Women of Trachis.* [301]

All of these perfections of Sophocles' poetry that have just been outlined are not traits that are isolated and self-sufficient; rather, they are different aspects and parts of a thoroughly integrated and completely blended whole. As long as the balance between vigor and law-governedness is not yet lost in the process of formation [*Bildung*], as long as the sum of beauty is not yet torn asunder, the particular could not be more perfect except at the expense of the whole. All the particular elements of excellence mutually abrogate to themselves a greater value in the thoroughly reciprocal interaction. From the unification of all these traits—of which I have only sketched the most general outline, essentially the outermost boundaries of its inexhaustibly rich essence—arises the *modest perfection,* the characteristic *sweetness,* which seemed to the Greeks themselves to be the truly characteristic traits of this writer. [302]

From a practical point of view, the merits of the different ages, the different types of poetry, and the different styles are very uneven. And although what is worthy of imitation in Greek poetry is disseminated everywhere, it nonetheless unifies itself within the midst of the golden age. From a *theoretical* [143M] point of view, however, the value of the *entire mass* is basically uniformly extraordinary.[102]

The *simple similarity* of the sum of Greek poetry contrasts very noticeably with the motley aspect and the heterogeneous mélange of modern poetry.

In general, Greek culture [*Bildung*] was utterly original and national, a whole complete unto itself, which attained an ultimate apex by means of mere inner evolution, and, having come around in a complete cycle, sank back into itself again. Greek poetry was just as original. The Greeks preserved the purity of their peculiarity and their poetry was consistently *national* not only in its initial beginnings but also in the course of its entire progress. It was *mythic* not just in its origins, but also in its entirety: for in an age of childlike culture [*Bildung*]—as long as freedom finds its inspiration only in nature and is not

[303]   self-sufficient—the different aims of humanity are not yet fixed, and its component parts are intermingled. Legend or *mythos* is, however, precisely that mixture wherein tradition and poetry join, where the presentiment of childlike reason and the dawn of fine art merge into one another. Natural culturation [*Bildung*] is simply the constant evolution of one and the same seed; the fundamental traits of its childhood will disseminate themselves over the whole and will be preserved by means of traditional customs and sacred institutions up until the end. Greek poetry is from its origins on—during the course of its progression and throughout its entirety—*musical, rhythmic,* and *mimic.* Only the arbitrariness of the manipulative understanding can forcibly separate what nature has eternally unified. A truly human predicament consists not solely of ideas or initiatives; it consists as well of a mixture of the two. It vents itself forth entirely, through all available openings, into all possible directions. It expresses itself simultaneously in arbitrary and natural signs in speech, voice, and gesture. In the natural development [*Bildung*] of the arts—before the understanding misconstrues its own rights, and confuses the limits of nature by its forcible intervention, destroying thereby its beautiful organization—poetry, music, and mime (which then was also rhythmic) are almost always inseparable sisters.

This similarity we apprehend not only in the whole but also in the

[304/144M] greater and smaller, coexisting or successive classes into which the whole divides itself. Despite the greatest disparity between the original artistic abilities and its judicious application, as well as that between the individual national character of the different peoples and the prevailing mood of the artist, the general relations between mind and nature are nonetheless unalterably and without exception determined in every great epoch of aesthetic development [*Bildung*]. In those epochs where public taste achieved the highest level of development [*Bildung*] and, in the context of utmost perfection, all organs of art could express themselves simultaneously in the most complete and free way, the general relations of the original elements of beauty were clearly determined by the spirit of the age, and neither the greatest nor slightest degree of original genius, nor the peculiar development [*Bildung*] and mood of the poet, could make possible a single exception to this necessity.

While these coexisting circumstances rapidly changed, the spirit of a great master apportioned his beneficent effects throughout many ages, and yet without thereby crippling inventiveness or fettering originality. An excellent, peculiarly determined style can maintain itself with remarkable uniformity through a long series of artists. Nonetheless, the general[103] tendency of the individual aims for the objective. Thus the individual now and then limits the scope of the objective, yet it never eludes its legitimate rule. [305]

The different stages of the seriatim evolution separate themselves on the whole clearly and distinctly from one another, but in the constant flow of history the outermost boundaries melt—like waves in a stream—into one another. The boundaries of the coexisting modes of taste and of the types of art are thus all the more segregated from one another. Their makeup is thoroughly homogeneous, pure and simple, much like the organism of plastic nature—not like the mechanism of the technical understanding. According to an eternal and simple law of attraction and repulsion, the homogeneous elements coalesce, and rid themselves of everything foreign the more they organically evolve and develop themselves.

The entire mass of modern poetry comprises an incomplete beginning, whose interrelation can only be amended to completion within the imagination. The unity of this whole that is in part apprehended, in part imagined, is the artificial mechanism of a product brought forth by means of human diligence. The homogeneous mass of Greek poetry, however, is an independent, perfect whole, complete unto itself, and the simple integration of its rigorous interrelation comprises the unity of a *beautiful organization,* where [145M] even the smallest part is necessarily determined by the laws and the aims of the whole, and yet is nonetheless free and self-sufficient. *The patent orderliness of its evolution* betrays more than coincidence. The greatest as well as the smallest advance evolves by itself out of what has preceded it and it contains the complete embryo of the next stage. The *inner principles of the living formation [Bildung]* that elsewhere in the history of humanity are hidden lie here in plain view; they are clearly and precisely inscribed upon the outward form. Just as the [306] homogeneous elements coalesce in a genial manner into a sound organization throughout the whole totality by means of the intrinsic strength of the striving force, just as the organic embryo—thanks to the constant evolution of the formative drive—completes its cycle, grows vigorously, blossoms copiously, matures quickly, and wilts suddenly: so it is with every type of poetry, every age, every school of poetry.

The analogy permits us—and makes it necessary—to postulate that in

Greek poetry nothing is coincidental and simply forcibly determined by external influence. Indeed, it seems that even that which is the most insignificant, most unusual and—so it would seem at first glance—the most coincidental, has evolved necessarily according to internal principles. Greek culture [*Bildung*] began in a state of absolute crudity; and its cosmic situation was, in disposition and motivation, fostered to the utmost—which, in terms of aesthetic development [*Bildung*] at least, was never disturbed by harmful external influences. These motive causes explain the origin, the peculiar makeup, and the apparent fate of Greek poetry. The general relations of its parts, however, the outline of the whole, the specific boundaries of its stages and types, the necessary laws of its progression, can only be explained in light of internal principles, in light of the *naturalness of its development* [*Bildung*]. This development [*Bildung*] was nothing other than the most unfettered evolution of the most felicitous disposition—the general and necessary embryo of which is

[307] founded within human nature itself. The aesthetic development [*Bildung*] of the Greeks in Athens as well as in Alexandria was never artificial in the sense that the understanding would have organized the entire mass, directed all forces, determined the aim and direction of its course. On the contrary, Greek theory was not in any way associated with the praxis of the artist; at the most, theory was later the dogsbody of the artist. The *drive in its entirety* was not only the motive but also the *guiding principle* of Greek culture [*Bildung*].104

    Greek poetry is, on the whole, a *maximum and canon* of *natural poetry;* its every single product is the most perfect of its kind. With bold certainty the

[146M] outlines are simply sketched and then filled and completed with exuberant vigor; every formation [*Bildung*] is the *complete intuition of a genuine concept.* Greek poetry contains for all fundamental concepts of taste and art a complete specimen collection of examples, which are so surprisingly useful for theoretical systems that it seems as if formative [*bildende*] nature had condescended essentially to anticipate the wishes of the knowledge-seeking understanding. In it the *entire cycle of the organic evolution of art* is concluded and completed; the greatest age of art—where the faculty for beauty could express itself most freely and completely—contains the *entire gamut of taste.* All pure varieties of the different possible combinations of the elements of beauty have been exhausted;

[308] even the order of the succession and nature of the transitions are necessarily determined by internal laws. The *boundaries of its poetic types* are not constrained by arbitrary divisions and combinations; rather, they are produced and determined by formative [*bildende*] nature itself. The system of all possible pure poetic types—which includes the different varieties, the immature types of an unevolved childhood, and the simplest bastard types that are produced out of the confluence of all genuine poetry in the decadent age of imitation—has completely exhausted itself. It is an *eternal natural history of taste and art.*

It contains actually the *pure and simple elements* into which one must first prescind the motley products of modern poetry if one is to completely unravel its labyrinthine chaos. Every circumstance is so genuinely, originally, and necessarily determined that the character of every individual Greek writer is essentially a pure and simple *aesthetic elementary intuition*. One cannot, for example, explain *Goethe's style* more pointedly, vividly, and concisely than by stating that he is a combination of the styles of Homer, Euripides, and Aristophanes.[105] [309]

"But Greek poetry so often and so grievously offends our sense of propriety. Far removed from the nobler ethics of our sophisticated century, it does not match up to—even when it attains its greatest perfection—the old romances when it comes to magnanimity, propriety, shame, and delicacy. Is not the famed simplicity of its resolute products poor and uninteresting! The material is paltry, the execution is monotonous, the thoughts are trivial, the feelings and passions lack energy, and even the form—according to the stringent demands of our superior theory—is often incorrect. Greek poetry should be our model? When it has not even heard of the greatest object of fine art—a [147M] noble, spiritual love?" This is what many moderns will think. "Very many lyric poems sing the praises of the most unnatural excesses, and in almost all poems there stirs the spirit of unbridled sensuality, dissipated luxuriance, etiolated unmanliness. In the crude buffoonery of the vulgar Old Comedies everything that can scandalize good morals and good society appears to be blended together. In this school of all vices—where even Socrates is the subject of comedy—everything holy is made fun of, and everything noble is willfully ridiculed. Not only the most wanton excesses, but even effeminate cowardliness and placid maliciousness[106] are depicted here casually in cheerful colors and in a deceptively charming light. The immorality of the New Comedies only appears to be not as bad because it is more feeble and more insubstantial. However, the finagling of deceitful slaves and intriguing suitors, the excesses of foolish youths are essentially—despite the frequently changing combinations—the constant and ever-recurrent fundamental traits of the basic plot. Even in Homer the iniquitous self-interest of his heroes, the bald manner [310] in which the poet represents—essentially with praise or even indifference— unjust cunning and immoral might hardly corresponds with the great dignity of the perfect epopee: just as the frequent coarseness of material and expression hardly corresponds with the rhapsodic interrelation of the whole. The tragedy of revenge is not only the most perfect of the most dreadful of crimes; in the sophisms of passion vice is also instructed in accordance with fundamental principles. Whose heart is not outraged to see the matricide of Electra represented as more dazzling—and hence as mitigated—than abhorrent. In order finally to rob the more refined soul of every inner fortitude the horrible tableau usually concludes with the depressing prospect in the shadowy backdrop of an all-powerful and uncomprehending—and no doubt envious and misanthropic—fate."

Before I prescind this interesting complex of modern presumptuousness, ingenuous misunderstandings, and barbaric prejudices into its constituent elements, I must first state at the outset a few things about the single, valid, *objective principle of aesthetic criticism.* Following which it will not be a difficult matter to deduce the subjective origin[107] of the conventional principles of this pathetic satire.

[148M]   All assessments, be they laudatory or reproachful, can only achieve validity under two conditions. The standard by which one judges and values must be universal; the application of it to the object to be criticized must be conscientiously faithful, and the perception must be so perfectly accurate that it would stand up to every examination. Otherwise, the judgment is a simple ukase. One can already infer the extent to which our philosophy of taste and art [311] is still incomplete and sketchy from the fact that there has not even been a significant effort to establish a *theory of ugliness.* And yet beauty and ugliness are inseparable correlates.[108]

Just as beauty is the pleasing appearance of the good, so is *ugliness* the displeasing appearance of the bad. Just as beauty rouses the mind—by means of the sweet allure of sensuousness—to devote itself to spiritual pleasures: so here a hostile attack on sensuousness is the cause and element of ethical pain. Thus life in all its charm invigorates and refreshes us, and even terror and suffering is fused with grace; while here the *disgusting,* the *grievous,* the *horrible* fills us with revulsion and abhorrence. Instead of graceful ease, a *clumsy awkwardness* oppresses us; instead of lively vitality, *dead weight.* Instead of a symmetrical tension in a beneficent alternation of movement and calm, a *painful rending* pulls one's interest to and fro in opposite directions. Where the mind longs for peace it is tormented by a *destructive rage;* where it yearns for movement, it is fatigued by *languorous weariness.*

In the representation of ugliness animalistic pain is only the element and organ of the *ethically bad.* Against the absolutely good nothing positive— [312] nothing absolutely bad—is posited; rather, only a mere *negation* of pure humanity, which encompasses totality and multiplicity.[109] Ugliness is also actually an empty pretense within the element of a real physical evil. Yet it is without moral reality. Only in the sphere of animality is there positive evil— *pain.* In pure spirituality only pleasure and painless limitation would occur; and in pure animality only pain and the gratification of *need without pleasure* [149M] would occur.[110] In the composite nature of man the negative limitations of spirit and the positive pain of the animal are thoroughly blended into one another.

The opposite of plentiful abundance is *emptiness,* monotony, uniformity, spiritlessness. Disparity and *struggle* are the opposite of harmony. *Wretched confusion* is opposed to actual beauty in the strict sense. *Beauty* in the *strict* sense is the appearance of a finite diversity in a conditioned *unity.* The *sublime,* however, is the appearance of the infinite—infinite abundance or infinite [313] harmony. It has thus a twofold antithesis: *infinite deficiency* and *infinite disharmony.*

The level of baseness is determined solely by the *degree of negation.* The level of ugliness, however, depends at the same time on the *intensive quantity of the drive* that is being contravened. The necessary prerequisite for ugliness is a deluded expectation, an aroused and then frustrated yearning. The feeling of emptiness and struggle can grow from mere discomfort to the most raging despair, even though the degree of negation remains the same and only the intensive strength of the drive increases.

Sublime beauty affords a complete pleasure. However, the result of *sublime ugliness* (which is a delusion that is made possible by an exertion of the drive) is *despair,* essentially an absolute, unmitigated pain. To this is added the *displeasure* (a sensation that plays a great role in the realm of the ugly) or the pain that accompanies the perception of individual ethical incongruities. For all ethical incongruities cause the imagination to augment the given material into the idea of an unconditioned disharmony.

In the strictest sense of the word, an *ultimate in ugliness* is obviously as impossible as an ultimate in beauty. It is just as unlikely that an unconditioned *maximum of negation*—or *absolute nothingness*—be present in any idea as that a maximum of affirmation obtain; even within the highest level of ugliness there is something beautiful. Indeed, even in order to present the ugly sublime and to create the appearance of infinite emptiness and infinite disharmony, the utmost amount of abundance and strength is required. The components of ugliness [314] struggle among themselves; and a contingent maximum (an objective, unsurpassable proximity) cannot—as is the case with beauty—be attained by means of the steady, albeit limited, vigor of the individual components and by means of the perfect law-governedness of the thoroughly unified components. Rather, only a *subjective* maximum can be attained: for there is for every individual receptivity a certain limit of disgust, suffering, despair, beyond which prudence [150M] will not go.

The artist should obey not only the laws of beauty but also the rules of art. He should not only avoid ugliness; he should also avoid *technical mistakes.* Every representational work of free art can bring censure upon itself in four different ways. Either the representation lacks representational perfection; or it sins against ideality and objectivity; or it sins against the conditions of its own inner possibility.

Incompetence lacks the implements and material that would correspond to the aim. *Clumsiness* does not know how to use the vitality and material that is at hand. The representation is then dull, vague, confused, and sketchy. *Falsehood* will confuse the eternal boundaries of nature and negate its own objective by means of *monstrous combinations of the genuine types of poetry*. A *healthy but nonetheless childlike culture* [*Bildung*] will simply lay out and outline its correct plan—without carrying it out—in *genuine but imperfect types of poetry*.

In the particulars the representation can be truly splendid; yet, on the whole, it will still negate itself through *inner contradictions;* it will destroy the conditions of its inner possibility, and do injury to the laws of *technical accuracy*. [315] When the vague mass of a supposed work of art utterly lacks permanence and the laws of inner possibility, or when the work could be essentially limitless and could not at all—or not rightfully—be separated from the rest of nature, one could term it *noninterrelation*. For it should actually be a small, closed-off world, a whole complete unto itself.

The *ideality* of art is contravened when the artist deifies his instrument, and when he foists representation—which should be only a means—into the place of the absolute goal, and strives[111] only for *virtuosity*. It is contravened by *affectation*.

The *objectivity* of art is contravened when, in the course of a universally valid representation, peculiarity gets involved, or quietly sneaks in, or flagrantly outrages. It is contravened by *subjectivity*.

This general outline of the pure types of all possible technical mistakes contains the first *basic principles of a theory of incorrectness,* which, together with the theory of ugliness, comprises the complete *aesthetic criminal code* that I would like to establish in the following *apology for Greek poetry*.

Greek poetry does not require rhetorical praise; the dodge of glossing over or of denying its real mistakes is entirely unworthy of it. It requires strict [316/151M] fairness: for even harsh reproach will be less disadvantageous to its honor than blind enthusiasm or indulgent indifference.

Every sensible person will readily admit the imperfection of the oldest types of Greek poetry as well as the artificiality of the later types of Greek poetry. Every sensible person will acknowledge the childlike sensuousness of the epic age, the luxurious excesses toward the end of the age of the lyric, and especially the frequent and dreadful severity of the older tragedies in the third phase of the dramatic age. A languorous turmoil follows the rapture that elevated the sensuously pleasurable—which should only be the animator and element of spiritual pleasure—to an ultimate objective. Then comes a resigned weariness and, finally, in the age of affectation and scholarly imitation, the ponderous aridness of a lifeless mass patched together out of individual fragments.

From the moment that representation elevated itself from the raw expression of a necessity to free play, the overall tendency of the entire striving force aimed for beauty. But *natural evolution could* not leap over any necessary stages of development [*Bildung*] and could *only progress gradually.* It was *natural, indeed necessary,* that Greek poetry subsided from the highest pinnacle of perfection *into the most profound decadence.* The drive that directed Greek culture [*Bildung*] is a powerful mover but a blind leader. If one places a diversity of blind motive forces in free association with one another without unifying them through a perfect law, they will ultimately destroy themselves. Thus it is with unfettered culturation [*Bildung*]: for here something foreign is taken up in the legislation itself because the amalgamated drive is a combination of humanity and animality. Since the latter achieves existence sooner and instigates the evolution of the former, it has the upper hand in the earlier stages of culturation [*Bildung*]. It retained this advantage in Greece among the great mass of the thoroughly uncultured [*ungebildeten*] citizens or citizenesses of [317] cultured [*gebildeter*] peoples as well as among the nations that had remained uncouth. And indeed a mass—but only the smaller mass that rules over the greater mass—became mature and independent. This greater mass constantly exerted a strong attractive force—which was strengthened by the infectious influence of slaves who had been thoroughly integrated by the surrounding barbarians—to pull the more refined mass down to itself. If there is no external constraint, and it is left to itself, the striving force can never stand still. Thus when, in the course of its gradual evolution, it reaches the era of a contentment that is uniform, limited in strength, but in its scope complete and regular—it will necessarily desire greater content even at the cost of harmony. Culturation [*Bildung*] will irretrievably sink into itself, and the pinnacle of its greatest perfection will come close to bordering on a distinct decadence. Only the [152M] guidance of an art produced by an understanding matured by vast experience could have lent the course of culturation [*Bildung*] a more felicitous direction. The lack of a *sound guiding principle*—which should define the greatest beauty and ensure for culturation [*Bildung*] a steady progression to the good—is not the misdeed of a single era. If a reproach can be leveled at that which is necessarily and actually the *fault of humanity itself,* then this is true of the whole of Greek culture [*Bildung*].

Yet this gradual emergence and this collapse into itself on the part of the entirety of Greek culture [*Bildung*], as well as of Greek poetry, does not at all contradict the assertion that Greek poetry is the *sought-after intuition* by means of which an objective philosophy of art in its practical as well as its theoretical aspects could first become useful and pragmatic. For a complete natural history [318] of art and taste encompasses the imperfection of the earlier stages as well as the decadence of the later stages—the constant and necessary chain of which no link can be skipped in the complete cycle of its gradual evolution. Objectivity characterizes the whole, and even those works whose style is reproachable are *solitary* and *legislative intuitions* that are valid for all ages due to the simple authenticity of the natural dispositions and limits, the bold certainty of the clear outlines, and the vigorous perfection of formative nature. The childlike sensuality of earlier Greek poetry had more uniform breadth and more beautiful proportions than the most artificial refinement of uncultivated [*mißbildeter*] barbarians. Even Greek affectation has its classical objectivity.

There is a certain type of dissatisfaction that is a clear indication of barbarism. Thus those who are not satisfied that Greek poetry is beautiful impose upon it an entirely foreign standard of evaluation; and in their confused pretensions they thoroughly mix together everything objective and subjective and demand that it should be more *interesting*. Certainly, even that which is most interesting could be more interesting, and Greek poetry is no exception to this universal law of nature. All quanta are infinitely progressive, and it would be a miracle if our poetry—enriched as it is in content by the advances of all [319]   the previous ages—did not surpass Greek poetry.

On the whole, the relation between men and women among the moderns is perhaps at least more felicitous—and the education of women slightly better—than it was among the Greeks. For the moderns, *love* was for some time—and, to some extent, even today—the only resort for every spontaneous [153M]   outburst of nobler feeling that would otherwise be dedicated to virtue and the fatherland. Even the poetic arts of the moderns owe a great deal to this propitious motivation. Admittedly, however, too often wild fancy and bombast are foisted upon genuine feeling, and the simplicity of nature is desecrated by means of an ugly and false shame. Certainly, the sublimated mysticism and the orderly, scholastic pedantry in the metaphysics of love of many modern writers are far removed from genuine grace. The desperate convulsions of the sick make more noise than the quiet but strong life of the healthy. The profound ardor of the faithful Propertius[112] unifies genuine vigor and delicacy and allows us to intuit much that was worthwhile of Callimachus[113] and Philetas.[114] And yet, in the age in which he lived, perfect lyric beauty was no longer conceivable. However, enough traces are at hand in order to be able to conjecture very precisely what and how much we have lost in the songs of Sappho, Mimnermos, and a few other erotic poets from the golden age of lyric. The gentle warmth, the urbane grace, and the liberal humanity that breaths in the erotic representations of the Attic New Comedy lives in many dramas of Plautus and Terence. On the other hand, when it comes to tragedy, the Greeks perhaps were justified in reproaching Euripedes. What should have been the momentary [320]   outpouring of feeling, or the quiet enjoyment of complete rapture, can only be stretched out to a tragic passion through the use of ugly, immoral, and fantastic adjuncts. Love plays only a subordinate role in many of the most splendid modern tragedies.

It would be no unpardonable crime if Greek poetry—due to a peculiarity of its otherwise singularly propitious situation—were in this matter somewhat backward. In general, adhering to the coincidental and not perceiving what is truly essential betrays a petty perspective. The artist does not need to be *everything to everyone*. Moreover, if he only obeys the necessary laws of beauty and the objective laws of art, he has unlimited freedom to be as peculiar as he wants to be. Because of an odd misunderstanding, one often confuses aesthetic *generality* with the universality that is absolutely indispensable. Only a *perfect insipidity* could make the utmost generality of a work of art possible. In an ideal representation the particular is the indispensable element of the general. If all the vigor that is peculiar to it dissipates, then even generality loses its effectiveness. Fine art is essentially a language of the godhead that divides itself into so many distinct dialects according to the variety of the types of art, the instruments, and the material. If the artist is worthy of his noble mission, and if　[154M] he simply speaks *divinely*, then he is free to choose the *dialect* in which he wants to speak. It would not only be irregular but also very dangerous to want to restrict him in this matter; for language is a web of the finest connections. It must, so it would seem, retain its characteristic features in order to be meaningful and apposite: in all events, a general, universal language that would be everything to everyone has still not been invented. The artist may also speak *with whomever* he finds suitable—with his entire people, or with just anyone,　[321] with the entire world, or just with himself. Yet he must and *should* address himself to a *nobler humanity* and not to the animality within the human individuals who are his public.

If it had only discovered the secret of the Greeks, the individuality of modern poetry would be at liberty to be objective within the individual. Instead, it wants to elevate its conventional idiosyncrasies to the status of a natural law of humanity. Not satisfied being the slave of so many aesthetic, moral, political, and religious prejudices, it also wants to clap its Greek sister in similar chains.

If the conventional rules of modern *decency* are valid laws of fine art, then Greek poetry is not to be saved; and if one wants to be logical, one must deal with it as[115] the monks did with the nudes of antiquity. Decency, however, has no command over poetry; it is not under its jurisdiction at all. The bold nudity in the life and art of the Greeks and Romans is not animalistic crudity but, rather, uninhibited naturalness, liberal humanity, and republican candor. The feeling of *genuine shame* was with no people more inherent and innate as with　[322] the Greeks. The source of genuine shame is ethical restraint and modesty of heart. False shame, however, arises out of animalistic fear, or out of affected prejudice. Its telltale signs are pride and envy. Its furtive and hypocritical essence betrays a deep consciousness of inner filth. Its false delicacy is the ugly makeup of depraved slaves, the effeminate finery of enfeebled barbarians.[116]

The objections against the *morality* of Greek poetry seem more important. Who would want to gloss over or consider trivial what would necessarily do injury to a pure mind? Yet whoever wants to have a say in this ought not be of such a sour temper that he would take offense at the exquisite näiveté with which the mischievousness of the newborn god in the *Hymn to Hermes* is represented.[117] Clearly, the objection contains some valid points. Yet the actual

[155M] perspective, the true context upon which everything depends appears to be missing. Before all else, one should distinguish the essential and coincidental ethicality and unethicality of a work of art. Only what is actually bad and *appears* as such and whose impression must necessarily affront every ethically noble feeling is *by its nature aesthetically unethical*. The appearance of the bad is ugly, and a basic aesthetic ethics (*ethics* in general is the predominance of pure humanity over the animality present within the faculty of desire) is therefore a necessary element of perfect beauty. The sensuality of early Greek poetry and

[323] the excesses of later Greek poetry are not only a moral but also an aesthetic deficiency and impropriety. It is, however, truly remarkable how profoundly the Attic people sensed their own decline, and with what vehemence the Athenians therefore accused and hated certain opulent writers—such as Euripedes,[118] or Cinesias[119]—who simply guessed at their own wishes or who followed the strongly flowing current of the whole.

There are Greek errors that modern writers are safe from. It is no great accomplishment to keep in line and in good discipline and order a docile force by means of the most forceful constraint. However, where people's proclivities[120] are not unrestrictedly free, morals[121] can be neither good nor bad. Whoever is merely indignant at the mischievous wantonness of Aristophanes betrays not only the limitations of his understanding, but also the incompleteness of his ethical disposition and development [*Bildung*]. For the lawless excess of this writer is not merely alluringly charming because of the sumptuous abundance attendant upon the most opulent of lives, but it is also—due to the unfettered activity of a surfeit of bubbling wit, overflowing spirit, and ethical vigor—breathtakingly beautiful and sublime.[122] Something is *coincidentally aesthetically unethical* when its baseness does not appear but—due to its very nature, and under certain subjective conditions of temperament and the association of ideas—can become the motivation for a definite unethical mode of

[324] thought or action. What could not become corrupted by coincidental circumstances, no matter how splendid it was? We give the ambiguous praise of complete innocuousness only to what is an absolute nullity. A work of art no longer exists if its organization is destroyed or if it is not apprehended; the effect

of the dissipated material no longer concerns the artist. Moreover, we are not warranted in expecting scientific truth from the poet. The tragedian often can not avoid[123] glossing over crimes. He requires strong passions and terrible events and he should present the morals of his characters in as beautiful and sublime a manner as the law of the whole will allow. Whoever is led to crimes [156M] by the example of an Orestes, a Phaedra, has probably himself just as much to blame as he who takes as his model the presumptuous suitor, the ingenious conman, and the charming freeloader from comedy! Indeed, a writer himself can have an unethical intention and his work can nonetheless still be ethical.[124]

Unarguably, the passionate fervor of decadent tragedy, the silliness of comedy, the opulence of the later lyric *accelerated* the decline of Greek morals. The simple effect of the representational arts had *reinforced* the already distinct ethical decadence of the culture, and it thus declined with *redoubled* speed. Yet this comes exclusively under the jurisdiction of a *political assessment,* which encompasses the[125] whole totality of human development [*Bildung*]. *Aesthetic* [325] *judgment,* however, isolates the development [*Bildung*] of taste and art from its cosmic context; and in such a realm of beauty and representation only aesthetic and technical laws are valid. Political judgment is the highest of all perspectives: . the subordinated perspectives of moral, aesthetic, and intellectual judgment are *all equal.* Beauty is an element that is just as primordial and essential to the duty of humanity as ethics.[126] All these coexisting elements should be in relations of *legal equality* (isonomy), and fine art has an inalienable right to *legitimate independence* (autonomy). The regnant force, which guides and organizes the entirety of human development [*Bildung*], must remain true to this fundamental law: otherwise it itself destroys the foundation upon which the right of its rule solely rests. It is the duty of the *political faculty* to organize into a unity all the scattered forces of the entire mind as well as all the individuals of the entire species. *Political art* may to this end limit the freedom of the individual without, however, damaging this fundamental law; but only under the condition that it does not hamper the progressive evolution and does not make impossible a future perfected freedom. It must essentially strive to make itself superfluous. [326]

The presumptions of *correctness* can confirm to what degree one is accustomed to misjudge the boundaries of the *poetic spheres.* When the critical anatomist destroys the beautiful organization of a work of art, analyzes it into elementary masses, and conducts then various physical experiments on the basis of which he proudly reaches conclusions, he deceives himself in a very obvious way: for the work of art no longer exists. There is no poem within [157M] which one could not demonstrate the presence of inner contradictions: but inner contradictions that do *not appear* do not harm technical truth; poetically they do not exist. Earlier French and English critics especially have often wasted their acumen on such wrongheaded nit-picking, and I am not certain as to whether echoes of this mannerism are still to be found here and there in Lessing. In general I believe that—with all due respect for theory—one accomplishes more in such an undertaking with the *sense as to what is fitting* than with the theory of what is fitting. The suspicion that the Greeks may have been slightly superior to other peoples in this regard must make us, at the least, very careful in reproaching them.

[327]   The passionate adherents of correctness are just as wrong when they demand, without regard for beauty and in accordance to the principle of virtuosity,[127] a *maximum of artificiality;* or when they simply reproach types of poetry, which are limited but are not unnaturally composed and which are instead naturally genuine and perfected in their limited way. Art, however, is simply the medium of beauty, and every natural type of poetry in which this objective—even if it is under certain restrictions—can be attained, is useful in its place. Naturally, a great deal of difference is to be found among the different types of poetry in terms of the degree of strength and compass; but only the monstrous mixtures and the immature types—if they arise out of the weakness of the artist, and are not grounded in the necessary catenation of culturation [*Bildung*]—deserve unconditional censure.

    The usual objections against *aphorisms* and especially against the *treatment of fate in Attic tragedy* present a remarkable example as to the extent to which one has to be on one's guard against the imperceptible yet powerful influences of the subjective upon aesthetic judgments. The scientific development [*Bildung*] of the Greeks was in general far behind ours, and dramatic poetry had to philosophize sparingly in order to remain popular. For this reason, the philosophical aphorisms of the tragic chorus are almost always uncertain and confused, indeed, very often trivial and frequently utterly wrong. Certainly, fundamental ethical errors can be derived out of many of them by

[328]   means of a chemical process similar to the one I have described above, errors which, if they were to be carried out rigorously, would not be compatible with the purest ethics. I must repeat again that everything that does not *appear* is situated beyond the *horizon of aesthetics*. Variety, correctness, and complete specificity of thought do not count for anything in the poetic arts. Philosophi-

[158M]   cal interest is dependent upon the degree of the intellectual development [*Bildung*] of the receptive subject, and is thus[128] *local* and *temporal*. Only the basic attitude has to be in itself as *sublime and beautiful* as the conditions of technical correctness allow and it has to be utterly appropriate for its context. The return into itself must be instigated by a departure out of itself that has already taken place; the *contemplation* must be *motivated* and it must strive to[129] mediate the struggle between humanity and fate and to *sustain* the equilibrium of the whole. If a beautiful sensibility were to express its presentiments of divine things in a preexisting language of images it would no doubt wreak endless havoc in science; for the representational arts, however, it is advantageous rather than disadvantageous.

The treatment of *fate* in the tragedies of Aeschylus leaves an even greater harmony to be desired. The satisfaction Sophocles provides, however, is always as perfect as it can be without destroying poetic truth—that is, the inner possibility. If the final resolution of the whole is not a glowing victory for [329] humanity, it is at least a *honorable retreat.* Yet he naturally mixes nothing into his representation that cannot be represented or that cannot appear. He attempts to resolve every dissonance and to afford complete satisfaction—not by means of the undisputed divinity of a nature that lies beyond the eternal veil no mortal can peer through but, rather, by means of the visible divinity of man. The realm of God lies beyond the aesthetic horizon and is only an empty shadow lacking spirit and vigor in the world of appearance.[130] Indeed, the poet who dares to arouse our indignation by means of outrageous baseness or an outrageous discrepancy between fortune and goodness—and who then believes that the paltry satisfaction derived from the prospect of evil punished or from a gesture toward some such world absolves him of any further responsibility—betrays but a minimum of artistic wisdom.[131] [330]

"It is true," one could think: "an ancient tradition states, and constantly repeats, that the imitation of the Greeks is the only way to reestablish a genuine, beautiful poetry.[132] Extensive experience has refuted this through the most diverse, yet entirely unsuccessful, attempts. One only has to go through the great number of artificial imitations that can be found in any library (for that is their actual home) and that are composed according to those models. Shadowy beings that lacked both permanence and independent vitality, they all died a wretched death sooner or later. Precisely those modern poems that contrast most decisively with the Greek manner are still alive, animate and [331/159M] thriving with the vigor of youth; they are full of genial originality—despite all their eccentric errors."

The fault lies not with Greek poetry but with the *manner and method* of the imitation, which—as long as national subjectivity rules, and as long as one strives only for the interesting—must necessarily end up one-sided. Only he who thoroughly knows Greek poetry *can* imitate it. Only he who appropriates for himself the objectivity of the entire mass, the beautiful spirit of the individual poets, and the perfect style of the golden age, can *truly* imitate it.

The separation of the objective from the local in Greek poetry is fraught with infinite difficulty. Both are not divided into self-sufficient masses; instead, they are thoroughly fused into one another. The objective disseminates itself into the finest twig of this many-branched tree; everywhere, however, something individual is mixed in as element and organ. Up until now that which was individual within the Greek forms and organs have been imitated only too often. One modernized the ancients in that one transposed the principle of the interesting to their poetry, or ascribed an authority to the Greek theory of art or to individual favorite writers that was due only to the spirit of the entire mass. Or one ascribed to them an authority even greater than that which would be consistent with the rights of genius, of the public, and of theory.

[332]

The *earlier didactic poem* of the Greeks, like those of Theognis,[133] the works of the physiologists and gnomists,[134] finds its true place only in the mythic ages of poetry. For at that point philosophy had not yet entirely disentangled itself and clearly separated itself from the mythos out of which it arose. Rhythm could still be the natural element of tradition; and poetic language— before the development [*Bildung*] of prose—could remain the universal organ of every nobler spiritual communication. With this transient relation the naturalness and the legitimacy of these forms ceases; what remained in the scholarly age of art for the *later* didactic poem of the Greeks was only the utterly nugatory principle of intentionally exhibiting the artificiality of vain virtuosos within difficult material. The possibility of an actually beautiful didactic poem of good form—that is, an ideal representation of a didactic material that is aesthetically informed—is thereby not denied; and here is not the place to determine whether some Platonic dialogues are poetic philosophemes or philosophical poems. But enough! None of these are to be found among the actual so-called didactic poems of the Greeks.

[160M/333]

Even the *Greek epos* is only a local form, about which one deluded oneself into believing strange things. This immature type of poetry is only in its proper place in an age where there is still no developed history and no perfect drama; where heroic legends are the only history; where the human nature of the gods and their dealings with heroes is a general popular belief of the people. One can easily understand that a people could become childish with age:[135] it is only because the epic poetry of the Greeks had attained such a highpoint of accomplishment in the age of myth that even the *epic devices of the Alexandrians and Romans* still have some basis and foundation. Poetry and mythos were the origin and source of all of the culture [*Bildung*] of antiquity; the epopee was the actual highpoint of mythic culture [*Bildung*]. Even the scholarly poet of the subsequent age encountered a determined material, formed implements. The receptivity was prepared; everything was organized; nothing could be forced. Without any support, however, modern epopees hover isolated in empty space. Great geniuses have squandered Herculean power in the attempt to create out of nothing an epic world, a felicitous mythos. The tradition of a people—the national fantasy—can perhaps further shape and idealize a great spirit, but it cannot metamorphize it or create it out of nothing. The Nordic fable, for example, is unarguably among the most interesting of antiquities: the poet, however, who wanted to revive it[136] either would have to remain commonplace and superficial or—if he wanted to be individual and precise—would be in danger of having to provide a commentary on himself. [334]

In vain we hope for a Homer; and why should we of all things wish for a Virgil, whose artificial style remains so far removed from perfect beauty? All attempts to organize the *Romantic poem* in a manner similar to the Greek and Roman epopee have failed. Tasso fortunately got stuck halfway there, and did not stray too far from the Romantic style.[137] And yet it is only individual passages—certainly not the composition of the whole—that make him the favorite poet of the Italians. A quiet *persiflage*—which often became loud enough—joined very much at the outset the gigantic dimensions, the fantastic life of the romantic poem. This has remained the enduring character of this type of poetry from Pulci[138] to the *Ricciardetto;*[139] and Wieland, who nuanced in a different—and always in a surprisingly new and always felicitous—manner the gradations of this whimsical mixture in every one of his romantic poems; yet he remained completely faithful to it. This was clearly no coincidence.[140] Romantic fable and romantic costume would have had to have been in their original form [*Bildung*] more purely human and beautiful in order to be able to become the felicitous subject matter of a tragic, beautiful, and simply organized epos. To what extent did Tasso[141] exclude whatever did not corre- [161M/335] spond to the demands of modern critics with regard to a well-ordered epopee?[142] Only those poets who do not entirely remove themselves from the prevailing sphere of national fantasy truly *live* in the mouths and hearts of their nation. However, poets who proceed in an entirely arbitrary manner encounter the sad fate of rotting in libraries until some day—and what a rare occurrence this is!—a man of letters turns up who has a sense for beauty, and who knows how to find and value the genuine talent that is buried here. And have the most capricious attempts to metamorphize the romantic fable or Christian legend into an ideal beautiful mythos succeeded? No!

"Naturam expelles furca; tamen usque recurret."[143]

It was and remains impossible to endow the barbaric mass with a Greek soul.[144] Tragic tension can no doubt be fostered, even if felicitous proportion, [336] graceful harmony—in short, *beautiful organization*—are missing from that which is wonderful, vigorous, and charmingly lively. Yet it cannot endure long enough, nor can it be spread uniformly in simple purity over a large whole without monotony and indifference. Eccentric greatness has an irresistible longing for that which is furtherest removed from it. Only by means of a beneficent merger with parody does tragic fantasy acquire bearing and perma-

[337]   nence. The strange combination of the tragic and the comic turns into the peculiar beauty of a new, charming hybrid formation [*Bildung*]. This combination is not in any way intrinsically monstrous nor is it in itself illicit. Indeed, it falls quite short of the pure types—especially the tragic type—when it comes to vigor and coherence: but no form in which the aim of representational art—beauty—can be attained, no form that was not mechanically constrained but was, rather, produced organically by means of plastic nature is fundamentally reprehensible. This is because the constraints, which restrict every form, are here more narrowly defined. Indeed, even all the diverse variations have fewer claims; nonetheless, they have full civil rights in the realm of art. It is surprising how much the most charming outgrowth of modern poetry—despite the extent to which the outward local form may vary—agrees with a variety of Greek poetry in its essential character. According to Greek technology, the romance is a *satyric epic*. In Attic drama the original raw energy of actual nature—in which opposed elements are thoroughly fused into one another—

[162M]   was separated into tragic and comic energy, and these were so mixed together anew so that the tragic had a slight predominance:[145] for in the case of absolute

[338]   equilibrium the two opposed forces would cancel themselves out in their convergence. Out of this arose the variety of satyric dramas, of which only a few of mediocre artistry and bad style remain. The dramatic sketches of the Dorians never raised themselves to the level of that distinction; and the natural, joyful wit of the Dorians was only subjective, local, and lyrical, never objective and truly dramatic.[146] Yet in the still composite and raw energy of the Doric mimes the comic still predominated. If we still had Homer's *Margites*,[147] some satyric dramas of Pratinas[148] or Aeschylus,[149] some outpourings of the Doric temper in the mimes of Sophron[150] or Rhinthon's *hilarotragoidia*,[151] then we would probably possess in them a standard by which we could evaluate. At least we would have the basis upon which to draw an interesting parallel to the charming grotesques of the divine master Ariosto,[152] and to the joyful magic of Wielandian fantasy. That which is *fitting* eluded the earnest men who wanted to idealize the fantastic magic of the romance into a tragic epic. Even the epic Thalia[153] of the moderns—the romantic *aventure*[154]—cruelly revenged itself on those who held it in contempt: for before the eyes of the entire public—who

[339]   suspected nothing—it transformed itself into farce.[155]

   Difficulties similar to those in the epic are attendant upon the use of mythic material in *tragedy*. It is not appropriate wherever there are native fables. For a foreign or outdated fable there remains only the choice between platitudes and learned incomprehensibility. Historic or invented material shackles the poet as well as the public to an incredible extent. Its heavy burden oppresses the free development [*Bildung*] of the whole. How much effort would it take to orient the public and to acquaint it provisionally with what remains unknown to it? The Greek tragedian could—by means of a myth that was universally known—go directly to the task at hand. The more unfettered attentiveness of the public was, of its own accord, more directed to the form; it did not cling so slavishly to the weighty mass. It is, in fact, a true Herculean task to poeticize thoroughly a still utterly raw material, to expand the petty detail into simple and great outlines, and especially to purify the indissoluble mixture of nature in accordance with the specific, ideal style of tragedy. The necessary equilibrium between form and material has been made so endlessly difficult for the modern tragedian that doubt could almost be raised as to whether a beautiful tragedy is actually still possible.[156] In our artificial culture [*Bildung*], moreover, every peculiar style becomes confused and effaced. Yet it appears necessary that nature itself mark out with a firm hand the path for the dramatist, and mitigate the division between the tragic and the comic.[157] I am pleased here to be able to point to a German example, which has raised great hopes and which quells all apprehensive doubt. *Schiller's* natural genius is decidedly tragic—in much the same manner as Aeschylus, whose bold outlines formative [*bildende*] nature appears to have dashed off suddenly in a moment of great enthusiasm. He reminds one that it seemed impossible to the Greeks that the same poet could compose both tragedies and comedies.[158] In *Don Carlos,* admittedly, the vigorous striving for beauty of character, as well as the beautiful organization of the whole is held in check or even suppressed by its colossal weight and the artificial clockwork of the composition: but the intensity of the tragic energy demonstrates not only the extent of the genial force, but its perfect purity attests also to the victory that the artist has achieved over the resistant material.[159]   [341]

  A book could easily be written about the confusion of the objective and the local in Greek poetry. I content myself with adding some brief observations to what I have already remarked upon.

  Prose and public oratory lay still in the cradle at the time of the most beautiful flowering of Greek *lyric.* Music as well as a rhythmic and mythic poetic language were the natural element for the outpouring of beautiful masculine or feminine feelings—in addition to being the actual organ of festive popular joy and communal enthusiasm. The lyric poet in general must, like the Greek poet, appear to speak his native language; the slightest suspicion that he has perhaps achieved his brilliance in borrowed public robes ruins all illusion and effectiveness. Regardless whether he portrays the condition of an individual temperament or an entire people: he must have a genuine *authorization* to speak. The situation portrayed must not be entirely feigned, but rather, it must   [342] at least find a genuine motivation in an already known object—no matter how unlimited the freedom of the poet in his treatment of it remains: for a lyric situation that was entirely invented could by itself be only the severed fragment

[340/163M]

of a drama; it must namely inhere an object that is just as invented as it is unknown, the presentation of which already infringes upon the sphere of drama.[160]

[164M]

The early Greek *epigram*, together with the *apologue*, finds its true place in the mythic age of poetry. The late Greek epigram, however, finds its true place in the age of affectation and decay.

If the interest of the *idyll* lies in the material and its contrast with the particular world the public lives in, then this comprises an absolute—and as such despicable—aesthetic heteronomy. Moreover, the epic or dramatic exposition of an originally lyric mood and inspiration is either a perversity on the part of the artist or a sure sign of the decay of art in general. If it is a question of the beautiful depiction of rural and domestic life, then Homer is the greatest of all the idyllic poets. One would have liked to have left the artificial imitations of naturalness to the Alexandrians.[161]

[343]

Voss's translation of Homer is splendid proof how faithfully and felicitously the *language* of the Greek poet can be reproduced in German.[162] His ideal is unarguably as carefully considered as it is perfectly executed. But woe to the imitator of the Greeks who allows himself to be led astray by the great translator! He is lost if he does not know how to separate the objective spirit from the local precisely at the point where they are most inextricably fused together.[163] The immortal work of the greatest historical artist of the moderns, the Swiss history of *Johannes Muller,* is planned and executed in the greatest Roman style. In the particulars, the work is completely infused with the genuine sensibility of the ancients: on the whole, however, it deteriorates again into the mannered, because the classical spirit, in addition to the individuality of antiquity, is affected. In the *Grammatical Dialogues Klopstock* clearly demonstrated, in a manner very different from Voss, how much the German language could achieve in the reproduction of Greek and Roman expression.[164] The examples are as varied as each in its own way is admirably perfect. Their simple excellence consists in being as true to the original language as possible in the most genuine, pure, powerful, and pleasing German.[165] Both

[344]

types seem to me equally indispensable for the general dissemination of genuine taste. Only when we have a classic translation of several of the greatest ancient poets in the style of Voss and Klopstock can we expect them to have a great influence upon and a profound transformation of the general taste.

One may commend the German language on the—albeit distant—similarity of its rhythmic development [*Bildung*] to *Greek rhythm.* Yet one

[165M]

should not deceive oneself about the limits of this similarity![166] Thus, for example, according to the principles put forth by the Greeks, a hexameter that takes up the trochee as an essential element can in no way be an epic meter—the style of which must necessarily be entirely vague in order that its permanence be truly unlimited.[167] The endless movement in a specific style, the epic use of a lyric rhythm, necessarily produces endless monotony, and exhausts finally even the most attentive interest. The musical principles of the rhythms of antiquity appear in general to be as absolutely different from those of the moderns as the character of Greek music—and as the Greek relation between poetry and music—is from ours. Even if under certain conditions Greek [345] rhythm is capable of being objective in a local element, that which is individual can have no authority for us—least of all can the theory upheld by Greek musicians be our model (although it is an indispensable aid for the correct elucidation of praxis and for the study of rhythm itself).[168]

A sort of illusory specter—which is worshiped as the actual *classicicity* by those who hope to become immortal by means of an artificial woodwork made of stilted phrases—has still not entirely disappeared. But nothing is less classical than affectation, overladen ornamentation, dispassionate splendor, and apprehensive thoroughness. The overly painstaking works of the scholarly Alexandrians already belong to the era of decay and imitation. Nonetheless, the most splendid products at their best are executed with care and keen judgment as well as with common sense; in addition, they are outlined with the greatest, indeed intoxicated, enthusiasm. The large number of works of the greatest dramatists already demonstrates that the amount of time and the extent of labor expended are not the standards by which one measures the worth of a work of art.[169]

Of the modern poets, only a few exceptions can be evaluated according to the degree to which they approximate the objective and beautiful. On the [346] whole, however, the *interesting* remains the actual modern standard of aesthetic worth. To extend this point of view to Greek poetry is to *modernize* it. Whoever finds Homer merely interesting, desecrates him. The Homeric world comprises a complete as well as easily understood portrait; the original magic of the age of heroes is infinitely enhanced in the mind that has become acquainted with the disorders of misculturation [*Mißbildung*], and has not yet entirely lost the sensibility for nature. It is easy for a dissatisfied inhabitant of our century to believe that he could find in the prospect of the charming simplicity, freedom, and sincerity of the Greeks everything that he has had to do without. Such a Wertheresque assessment of the venerable poet does not constitute a pure enjoyment of the beautiful, or a pure appreciation of art. Whoever delights in [166M] the *contrast* between a work of art and its particular world, actually *travesties* it in thought, regardless whether his mood be jocular or very earnest. Least of all may authority—on which only a complete, perfect, and beautiful intuition has a claim—be transposed to the one-sided, merely interesting assessment of a part of it.

One should not imitate just *any one,* or a particular, *favorite poet,* or the *local form or the individual organ:* for *an individual "as such" can never be a universal norm.* The modern poet who wants to strive for genuine, beautiful art should appropriate for himself the ethical abundance, the unfettered law-governedness, the liberal humanity, the beautiful proportions, the delicate equilibrium, the splendid appositeness that is more or less scattered over the entire mass. He should also approximate the perfect style of the golden age, the genuineness and purity of the Greek poetic forms, the objectivity of the representation—in short, the *spirit of the whole: pure Greekness.*

[347]

One cannot properly imitate Greek poetry as long as one does *not* actually *understand* it. One will only learn to elucidate it philosophically and to appreciate it aesthetically when one has studied it in *its entirety:* for it is such a profoundly interconnected whole that it is impossible to understand and judge accurately even the smallest part isolated out of its context. Indeed, all of Greek culture [*Bildung*] is of a piece, such that it can only be recognized and appreciated in its entirety. The historian of Greek poetry must bring, in addition to the natural talent of the art critic, the scientific principles and concepts of an *objective philosophy of history* and an *objective philosophy of art* in order to search for and find the *principles and organism* of Greek poetry. And everything depends on this.

It is true that a few great poets of antiquity are almost considered native sons by us. The public was certainly fortunate in its selection in that it chose well from those who are more easily grasped and who are by themselves—at least *to a certain extent*—more easily understood. Others—for whose heterogeneous individuality in form and organ no analogy can be found in the entire subjective sphere of the moderns, whose work must remain *entirely* incomprehensible to those who lack knowledge of the principles and the organism of Greek poetry in its entirety, and whose ideal heights exceed by far the narrowness of even the more refined regnant taste—could not become popular. Certainly, a complete knowledge of Greek art would neither be possible nor appropriate for every connoisseur, who perhaps only wants to cultivate [*bilden*] himself by means of the enjoyment of the beautiful. One may demand from the poet, from the expert, from the thinker—for whom it is a serious matter not just to know and to practice genuine fine art but also to disseminate it—that he not shy away from any difficulty: for it comprises an indispensable means to his objective. The works of Pindar, Aeschylus, Sophocles, Aristophanes are only studied passingly; they are even more poorly understood. Which means that the most perfect types of Greek poetry—and hence the era of the poetic ideal and the golden age of Greek taste—remain virtually unknown.

[348]

[167M]

Without a specific knowledge of its actual context, its proper place in the whole, something inappropriate must remain in even the most all-encompassing assessment of those popular poets. *Homer's* poems are the source of all Greek art. In fact, they are the foundation of Greek culture [*Bildung*] in general; they are the most perfect and most beautiful flowering of the most sensual age of art. Yet one should not forget that Greek poetry attained greater levels of art and taste. If there were a replacement for that which is irreplaceable, then *Horace* could to some extent console us over the loss of the greatest Greek lyric poets of that class that did not depict the public circumstances of an ethical totality in the name of the people but that sang of the beautiful sentiments of particular individuals. At the same time, he contains the most exquisite of the few entirely peculiar artistic products of the genuine Roman spirit that has come down to us. This "favorite poet of all educated [*gebildeten*] people" was always a great teacher of humanity and of a liberal way of thinking. His patriotic odes are a venerable memorial to the noble sensibility of the Romans and reminds one that even Brutus thought highly of the poet's civic virtues.[170] His beautiful lyric morality is either natural or it has been eagerly   [349] and spontaneously borrowed. But most of his songs, because they lack a graceful unity, sway back and forth between the Greek prototypes and the Roman inspiration. One should also not put much store by his erotic poems. Indeed, one can find in them individual traces of a charming philosopher and a worthy poet: but on the whole they are almost always wooden and, as the Romans might say, a little crass. And every now and then the choice of rhythms betrays the decay of musical taste. As to *Virgil,* I can not justify the excessive admiration accorded to him. I can, however, excuse it. For the friend of beauty his worth may indeed be slight; yet he remains an extremely remarkable study for the art critic. This learned artist chose individual parts and traits from the rich store of the Greek poets with something approximating taste, insightfully fused them together, and laboriously honed, polished, and groomed them. The   [168M] whole is a patchwork lacking a living organization and beautiful harmony. Yet he can nonetheless be regarded at the highest pinnacle of the scholarly, artificial age of ancient poetry. Admittedly, he lacks the ultimate polish and refinement of the Alexandrians, but by virtue of the lively Roman vigor of his poetic talent he by far outrivals the enervated Greeks of that age in their own style. In the context of this imperfect style, he is not perfect as such; but nonetheless he is the most outstanding.

The most unfortunate idea that anyone ever had—and many traces of its general prevalence still remain—was this: to attribute to *Greek criticism and art theory* an authority that, in the realm of theoretical science, is thoroughly unacceptable. One believed here to have found the actual *philosopher's stone of aesthetics*; isolated rules of Aristotle and epigrams of Horace were used as   [350] powerful talismans against the evil demon of modernity; it took some time for the tattered wretchedness of the initiates to arouse some suspicion about the authenticity of the mysteries.

The erroneous conclusion from which one proceeded were the words of *Hurd:* "The antients are our masters in the art of composition. Such of their writings, therefore, as deliver instructions for the exercise of this art must be of the highest value."[171] Nothing could be further from the truth! Greek taste was already completely decadent when theory still lay in the cradle. Theory cannot bestow talent. Greek theory never determined the purpose and ideal of the artist, who obeyed solely the laws of public taste. Even a perfected philosophy of art would not suffice to reestablish a genuine taste. Greek and Roman thinkers were, however (to judge from fragments, reports, and analogies), to so little extent in possession of a perfected system of an objective aesthetic science that there is no evidence of an attempt at, a sketch of—to say nothing of a persistent striving for—such a system. Not even the limits and the method were determined; not even the concept of a universally valid science of taste and art was defined. Indeed, even its possibility was in no way deduced.

Undeniably, the critical fragments of the Greeks contain important contributions to the explication of Greek poetry as well as excellent material for the [351] future realization and completion of such a system. Elaborate analyses, like those of Dionysius, are priceless, and even the smallest aesthetic judgment can have great value.[172] Applied concepts and determinations referred to *perfect intuitions* and could not be replaced simply by means of pure science. Judgments fell under the infallible guidance of a natural, properly attuned sen- [169M] sibility; with the Greeks, the capability to receive and appreciate beautiful representations was as perfect and unmatched as the capability to produce them. In general, in the theoretical portions of aesthetic science, subsequent critics—especially when it comes to questions of application and the particulars—are of the greatest value; in the practical portions of aesthetic science, the most general principles and concepts of the earlier philosophers especially are the most valuable.

The source of all Greek culture [*Bildung*] as well as of all Greek theory and science was *mythos.* Poetry was the oldest, and—before the beginning of oratory—the sole teacher of the people. The mythic way of thinking—according to which poetry in its true sense is a gift and revelation of the gods, and the poet is its holy priest and spokesman—remained at all times a popular Greek belief. The doctrines of *Plato* adhere to it and probably also those doctrines of *Democritus* on musical enthusiasm and the divinity of art. The popular (exoteric)[173] expression of Greek philosophy had in general a very *mythic* aspect. Just as in our time artists attempt to get themselves accepted as scholars and thinkers (since their actual worth would not count for much to the masses): so did the Greek philosopher tend to pass himself off as both a [352] musician and poet. The Platonic doctrine of the determination of art constitutes the most splendid Greek resource that has been passed down to us and which might be used for a practical philosophy of art. The practical philosophy of the earliest Greek thinkers was thoroughly *political*.[174] And this politics was, in its fundamental principles, far from being the slave of experience. Rather, it was utterly rational; yet, in its expression and in its organization, it generally kept to what was given and at hand. Greek philosophy never attained—like Greek art—that stage that is characterized by a *complete autonomy* of development [*Bildung*]. In Plato especially the organization of the whole is not determined internally but, rather, is formed [*gebildet*] and produced externally. In order to understand Plato's doctrine, therefore, one must know not only the mythic origin of Greek culture [*Bildung*] in general, but also the entirety of Greek political, moral, and philosophical culture [*Bildung*] to its fullest extent! In a slightly different manner, that which was widely accepted comprised the basis upon which all the doctrines of the *sophists*—even those on beauty and art—found their point of departure: it also comprised the point towards which they strove. In *Aristotle* theoretical aesthetics is still in its infancy, and practical   [170M] aesthetics is utterly in decline. His theory of the determination of art in the eighth book of the *Politics* gives proof of a liberal manner of thinking and a not entirely unworthy cast of mind: nonetheless, the perspective is already no longer political but, rather, only moral.[175] In the *Rhetoric* and in the fragments of the *Poetics* he treats art only *physically*, without any regard to beauty; he treats   [353] it in a merely historical and theoretical way. On the occasions where he now and then judges aesthetically, he expresses only a keen sense for the correctness of the structure of the whole, for the perfection and refinement of its integrity. How often one finds in Aristotle and in the later rhetoricians specific references to lost works, to things entirely unknown to us, and which are entirely incomprehensible or which can be deciphered only with great difficulty? Indeed, the whole is frequently composed in an idiosyncratic manner. Hence the main criterion by which Quintilian judges the worth of a poet is whether it serves to teach young orators to chatter in an affected manner.[176] The specific motivation of the critical epistles of *Horace,* the essence of their particular circumstances—their cosmic situation—is sometimes almost entirely unknown to us, and at other times in the main unknown.[177] Despite many probable or ingenious hypotheses, we fumble about completely in the dark.

All components must interact with one another in any consideration of an all-encompassing, complete knowledge of the Greeks; the study of the Greek theory of art is certainly an *integral part* of the complete study of Greek culture [*Bildung*] in general, or of aesthetic development [*Bildung*] in particular. But in the *methodology* of such a complete study Greek criticism ought to come very late in the program. One must already know the entire mass, the organism, and the principles of Greek poetry in order to be able to search for and find the pearls that lie hidden and for the most part unused in the critical writings of the Greeks.

I am far removed from the dictatorial presumptuousness, the despotic reforms of the supposed representatives of humanity, who lay plans for so [354] much—about which, moreover, not a word is to be found in their journals—and who[178] decree a great deal that would not be sanctioned by the public popular will, as expressed in the primordial assemblies of humanity. The claim that a universally valid science of beauty and representation as well as a correct imitation of the Greek prototypes is the necessary condition for the reestablish-[171M] ment of genuine, fine art, is so *well established,* that it is not even *new.* I content myself with the modest contribution of having traced aesthetic culture [*Kultur*], of having fortunately guessed the meaning of the history of art as it has been till now, and of having found a great prospect for the history of art that is yet to be. Perhaps, by seeking to determine the proper place of every noteworthy manifestation in the larger totality of the eternal laws of the development of art, I have succeed in illuminating some points of darkness, in solving some contradictions. It can be a testament to and a confirmation of the outline thus sketched that, accordingly, the struggle between ancient and modern aesthetic development [*Bildung*] becomes irrelevant; that the whole of ancient and modern art history surprises one because of its profound interrelatedness, and completely satisfies one because of its absolute purposefulness.

Every great, albeit eccentric, product of the modern artistic genius is, from this perspective, an authentic—and, in its place, very purposeful—advance; and as heterogeneous as the outward prospect may be—it is actually a true approximation of antiquity. The necessity of the stages of the gradual, seriatim evolution is no excuse for a weakness that does not measure up to the standard of an excellence that has already been attained. It is instead an explanation of and justification for the deficiencies and excesses of the truly great artist, who hastened a few steps ahead of the course of culturation [*Bildung*] [355] and sped up its evolution, and who could nonetheless still not leap over entire stages of culturation [*Bildung*].

The *history of the development* [*Bildung*] *of modern poetry* presents nothing less than the constant struggle between the *subjective disposition* and the *objective tendency* of the aesthetic faculty—and the gradual predominance of the latter. With every essential change of the relations between the objective and the subjective a new *stage of culture* [*Bildung*] begins. Modern poetry has already truly gone through two great periods of culturation [*Bildung*]—periods, which, however, do not follow upon one another noncontiguously but are rather joined to one another like links in a chain. Now it finds itself in the beginning of the third period. In the *first period,* the one-sided national character present throughout the entirety of aesthetic development [*Bildung*] had the decisive upper hand; and only now and then did a few isolated traces of the guidance of aesthetic concepts and the tendency toward antiquity rouse themselves. In the *second period,* the theory and imitation of the ancients ruled to a great extent the entire mass: but subjective nature was still too powerful to be able to obey fully the objective law; it was bold enough, however, to slip in under the name of the law. Such imitation and theory—and with it taste and [172M] art itself—remained one-sided and national. The resultant anarchy of all individual styles, of all subjective theories, and of the different imitations of the ancients, and the eventual effacement and destruction of one-sided nationality characterizes the *crisis of the transition* from the second to the third period. In the *third* period, objectivity is truly attained—at least in individual aspects of the entire mass:[179] objective theory, objective imitation, objective art, and objective taste. [356]

But the second period is concerned only with a *portion* of the whole: the beginnings of the third period are concerned only with *isolated parts* of the entire mass. And a significant portion of it has, up until now, been mired in the first stage. Yet still the aim of whole poetic types is nothing less than a true representation of the most interesting national life. Just as the national character of the peoples of Europe has already, in three distinct crises, experienced three great evolutions—in the age of the crusades, in the age of Reformation and the discovery of America, and in our century: so has the *national poetry of the moderns* flourished *three times* in three different epochs.

The situation of the aesthetic development [*Bildung*] of our present age made it necessary for us to survey all of the past. We now have returned to the point from which we started. The symptoms that characterize the crisis of the transition from the second to the third period of modern poetry are everywhere evident, and here and there the already *unmistakable beginnings of objective art and objective taste* are astir. Perhaps no moment in the history of taste and the poetic arts was as characteristic of the whole, so rich in consequences from the past, so pregnant with fertile seeds for the future. *The time is ripe* for an important revolution in aesthetic development [*Bildung*].[180] What can now only be guessed at will be known with certainty in the future: that in this important moment—which is part of other great crises[181]—the lot of true fine art will be decided on the scales of fate. Never could idle indifference toward beauty, or proud certainty about what has already been attained be more inappropriate; never could one expect a greater reward than that which presages the future course of the aesthetic development [*Bildung*] of the moderns. With satisfaction, if not with worshipful admiration, the following ages will look back on the present age. [357]

Aesthetic theory has reached the point where at least an *objective outcome*—turn out as it may—cannot be far. After the *pragmatic preliminary exercises* of the theorizing instinct (first period)—whose fundamental principle was *authority*—an actual *scientific* theory arose. Approximately at the same time the *dogmatic system of rational and empirical aesthetics*[182] developed and formed themselves (second period); and the antinomy of the various mannered theories led to *aesthetic skepticism* (crisis of the transition from the second to the third period). This was the preparation and motivation for the *critique of aesthetic judgment*[183] (beginnings of the third period). Yet the matter is far from concluded. The aestheticians themselves, who all took as their starting point the conclusions of critical philosophy, are unified neither in principles nor in method. Critical philosophy itself has not entirely brought to an end its persistent struggle with skepticism. There is, in general, as a great thinker has observed,[184] much left to do in the practical realm. Yet, since the foundation of a critical philosophy has been discovered thanks to *Fichte,* there is a sure principle by means of which to amend, complete, and carry out the Kantian outline of practical philosophy. There can be no serious doubt about the possibility of an *objective system of a practical and theoretical science of aesthetics.*

Even in the *study of the Greeks* in general and of Greek poetry in particular our age stands on the brink of a great phase. For a long time one knew the Greeks only through the medium of the Romans. Study of the Greeks was *sporadic* and *utterly lacking in philosophical principles* (first period); one then organized and directed this study—that was still sporadic—according to arbitrary hypotheses, or according to *one-sided principles,* and individual points of view (second period). The Greeks are already studied *in their entirety and without philosophical hypotheses*—rather, with disregard for all principles (crisis of the transition from the second to the third period). Only the last and greatest step is still to be undertaken: to organize the *entire mass according to objective principles* (third period). The chaotic wealth of all the individual elements and the struggle of the different opinions about the whole will necessarily lead to a search for and the discovery of a universally valid organization of the entire mass. Indeed, knowledge about the Greeks can never be brought to completion and the study of the Greeks can never be exhausted: yet a *fixed point* can be attained that can safeguard the thinker, the historian, the expert, and the artist from dangerous, fundamental errors, completely false perspectives, and absurd attempts at imitation.

"But you yourself," one could say, "put forward aesthetic vitality and morality as necessary postulates of the aesthetic revolution.[185] How then can something be determined ahead of time about the future course of culturation [*Bildung*], since these preliminary conditions themselves depend on a felicitous confluence of the most unusual circumstances? That is, it depends on an

[173M]

[358]

[359]

[174M]

approximation. Who has yet been able to learn from nature the sleight of hand by means of which it produces geniuses and brings forth artists? Certainly *aesthetic* genius, that rarest of all gifts, can be perfected slightly by means of cultivation [*Bildung*]—while running the risk of being falsified—but it can never be *created!* Also, for most individuals there seems to be a *natural,* unsurpassable *limit* in the compass and the vitality of ethics. Only a few independent exceptions are unlimited in their perfection. And don't these seem to owe their independence to the strange confluence of the most felicitous circumstances—to *coincidence?* The proud intellect of the rigorous thinker[186] will naturally not grant it, but an impartial assessment of the history of art appears to yield the following conclusion: nature is, on the whole, grudging and stingy with its most precious gifts; only now and then, in its finest moments, does it cast, according to whim, a handful of true artistic souls onto a favored land, in order that the light in this crepuscular world is not entirely extinguished."

Nothing can be determined as such about the future course of culturation [*Bildung*]: much, no doubt, can be conjectured about it. Conjectures to which one is compelled by the requirements of humanity, and which the laws of reason and history justify and establish. As if they had sat in counsel with the gods, they appear to know the secret intentions and drives according to which nature clandestinely operates. Science and history do not know as much as this. Yet they do know that the rarity of genius is not the fault of human nature but rather of an imperfect human art, *political bungling.* The freedom of humanity is fettered by its own perspicacity, which constrains the fellowship of culture [*Bildung*]. If, despite all of this, the stifled fire comes back to life, then it will be beheld as a miracle. Just let culturation [*Bildung*] do its work, and then see if it is lacking in vigor! Otherwise, why would always the slightest, momentary favor have wrested, as if by magic, such a majestic abundance of dormant forces out into the light of day? [360]

The necessary conditions of all human development [*Bildung*] are: vitality, law-governedness, freedom, and communality. Only when the law-governedness of aesthetic vitality is secured by an objective basis and style, can aesthetic development [*Bildung*]—by means of the *freedom of art* and *the communality of taste*—become thoroughly far-reaching and *public.* Genuine beauty must first have set secure roots in many different places before it can spread itself over the entire expanse, before modern poetry can attain the *next* [175M] *imminent* stage of its evolution: the *thorough predominance of the objective over the entire mass.*

One may not, however, set some requirements of aesthetic development [*Bildung*] aside while one completes the others. All four are in a *thoroughly reciprocal relation* with one another. It is, therefore, not too early to clear everything out of the way that could hinder *aesthetic communication.* Particu-

larly among *German* poets a very dangerous—in fact, illiberal—way of thinking predominates that sanctions as a fundamental principle the natural German inability to communicate. The sublime imperturbability of the German
[361]   nation, and the envious animosities of petty spirits often produce in creditable
but vain men a nasty mood, which can often harden into a malicious bitterness.
Sulking, they cloak their affronted pretensions in sneering pride, shut their
talent up entirely within themselves, or step only with a sour expression before
the public. Their mindset is so incapable of elevating itself above the limited
present, that it considers genuine beauty in general to be a *mystery,* and the
publicness of aesthetic development [*Bildung*] an impossibility. Only through
sociability is the raw peculiarity purified and mitigated, enthused and bright-
ened; the inner fire gently brought to light, the outward form rectified and
determined, completed, and intensified. Excessive solitude, however, is the
mother of strange caprices. Hence the clumsy severity, the brusque tone, the
somber complexion of many otherwise excellent German writers. Ultimately,
this course can deviate so far from the simplicity of nature, from the truly
essential, and from genuine beauty, that doubt could arise as to whether these
aesthetic mysteries might not be a *holy order without a secret,* where everyone
believes that the others know it.

For some time now the French have surpassed us by far in the *com-*
[362]   *munication* of knowledge, ethics, and taste. By these means, they could attain a
higher stage of perfection in *public Greek poetry* than other cultivated nations of
Europe. One will probably seek to explain such an unexpected phenomenon as
being due to the new political form—which may be nothing more than the
felicitous impetus that drove to fruition the force that has long lain dormant.[187] Where only a few individual beautiful traits—which could become
the main features and outlines of an ideal realization—are present in a precisely
determined national character; where musical and poetic talent are not entirely
lacking, where there is only a small degree of aesthetic development: a nobler
lyric must spontaneously arise[188] as soon as there exists *public morals,* a public
[176M]   will and public predilections, and a national soul and mood. The most decisive
and most limited one-sidedness is not intrinsically inhospitable to lyric
beauty—if only the lack of breadth is replaced, as was the case with the
Dorians, by unmitigated vitality and grandeur.

Drama that is to be beautiful requires a fully developed culture [*Bildung*]
and complete freedom from national limitations—characteristics the French
find themselves far from possessing! It could easily take centuries before they
attain this: for the new political form will only concentrate more intensely and
isolate more decisively the one-sidedness of its national character. Thus the so-
[363]   called French tragedy has also become a classical model of absurdity. It is not
only an empty formality without vigor, charm, or substance; rather, even its

form is an absurd, barbaric mechanism, without an inner principle of life and natural organization. The French national character can appear interesting and charming in the novel and in comedy, which satisfy themselves with the modest sphere of subjective representations; in the so-called tragedy of a Racine and Voltaire, however, the most infelicitous perspective on the French national character is idealized to the point of unbearability by means of a fruitless claim to objectivity. In the course of the constant alternation of the disgusting and fatuous, repugnant intensity and dull vacuity are intimately fused into one another.[189] In any case, the French, just like the English and Italians (the poetry of the latter two nations does not at the moment have to be attended to since they seek to anticipate the Germans!), lack an objective theory, and a genuine knowledge of the poetry of antiquity. In order to just get a clue about how to get on the path toward this, they would have to take lessons from the Germans. Which is a matter that they would come to a decision on only with difficulty!   [364]

In *Germany* and only in Germany have aesthetics and the study of the Greeks attained a level that must necessarily result in the total transformation of the poetic arts and taste. The most important advances in the seriatim evolution of philosophical aesthetics were the rational system and the critical system. Both were established and developed by *Germans*—the former by *Baumgarten, Sulzer,* and others; the latter by *Kant* and his successors.[190] The empirical system and skeptical system of aesthetics, on the contrary, were a necessary outcome of the general course of philosophy, rather than an actual discovery and contribution of certain English writers. In the older style of classical criticism, our *Lessing* surpasses by far his predecessors in England in terms of acuity and a genuine sensitivity for beauty. The *Germans* have brought   [177M] about an entirely new and incomparably higher level of the study of the Greeks; and it will probably remain their exclusive property for some time. Instead of the many names that could be given here, only one will be mentioned. *Herder* joins the most extensive knowledge with the most delicate feeling and the most supple sensitivity.[191]   [365]

Who can still harbor doubts about the poetic talents of German artists since the bold, inventive *Klopstock* became the founder and father of German poetry? Since the liberal *Wieland* embellished and humanized it? Since the astute *Lessing* purified and fortified it? Since *Schiller* gave it greater vigor and vivacity?[192] Through each of these great masters all of German poetry was generally inspired to a new life and strove with renewed strength ever more forcefully onward. How many other poets followed those initial innovators happily and yet in a peculiar way; or went their own—perhaps not less noteworthy—way, which, as a result, was less noticed because it did not   [366] coincide so well with the spirit of the age and the orientation of public culture

[*Bildung*]. *Bürger's* praiseworthy attempt to take art out of the stifling reading rooms of the scholars and out of the fashionable coteries and introduce it to the broader world, and to reveal the mysteries of the holy orders of virtuosos to the people, has had a most felicitous, enduring influence.[193]

How much ground would our single, important rival, the French,[194] have to cover before they could begin to suspect to what extent *Goethe* approximates the Greeks![195] Another sign of the approximation of antiquity in poetry is the remarkable tendency to employ the chorus in the greater lyric poems of *Schiller* (as in *The Gods of Greece* and the *Artists*). And Schiller is an artist, who one would think—because of his natural hatred of limitations—would be at the furthest remove from classical antiquity. As different as their outward appearance and substance may be, the similarity of this poetic style to that of Pindar's is unmistakable. Nature endowed him with intensity of sensibility, nobility of thought, magnificence of imagination, dignity of language, and authority of rhythm—in short, with the *heart and voice* that a poet should have who wants to grasp in his mind an ethical totality in order to depict the circumstances of a people, and to give expression to humanity.

[367]

[178M]

Beneath a heterogeneous exterior, exquisite passages of *Wieland's poetry* are to the same extent objective-comical and genuinely Greek. With surprise the connoisseur of Attic grace and genuine comedy often rediscovers here Aristophanes—and more often Menander.

There will be people—whose short-sighted vision is utterly incapable of any great historical perspective, who perceive in the detail only the detail, and who see everything as isolated—who will put forth petty objections against this great determination of German poetry. If, however, a felicitous impetus could suddenly transform the still slumbering capacity for communicability that is in German taste and German art into elastic activity: then even those onlookers who can only see the obvious will realize with surprised astonishment that the Germans surpass in particulars the most cultivated nations of Europe when it comes to the level of culture [*Bildung*] to the same extent that the Germans fall behind the same nations when it comes to the general and thorough dissemination of culture [*Bildung*].

Winckelmann spoke once of those *few* who still know the Greek poets. Should there not be now in Germany *a few more?* Will the number of those who strive for genuine art not increase further? With this hope I *consecrate* this essay and this collection to *all artists.* Just as the Greeks termed those who rhythmically organized the ethical bountifulness of their inner minds, and ordered it into harmony, *musicians;* thus I term those who love beauty "artists."

Appendix

Preface

A history of Greek poetry in its entirety encompasses also the history of   [205/77M]
oratory and the historical arts. The veracious history of Thucydides is, according to the correct judgment of a Greek expert, also a beautiful poem.[1] And in
the orations of Demosthenes, as well as in the dialogues of Socrates, the poetic   [206]
imagination is indeed limited by a specific aim of the understanding, but it is
not robbed of all freedom nor is it absolved of the duty to be beautifully at play.
For beauty should be; and every discourse, whose main or secondary purpose is
beauty, is entirely or in part poetry. It encompasses, moreover, the history of
Roman poetry, whose imitations must too often compensate us for the loss of
the original works. The history of Greek criticism as well as the fragments that
might be found of a history of Greek music and mime are as indispensable as
the knowledge of all of the legends about the Greek gods and of the Greek
language in all its branches and all its metamorphoses. Within the most hidden
depths of the history of morals and governments lies that by means of which
alone the contradictions and gaps in the history of art can be resolved and
augmented, the scattered fragments ordered, the apparent puzzle explained: for
the art, morals, and the forms of government of the Greeks are so thoroughly
interconnected that knowledge about them does not permit itself to be broken
up. In general, moreover, Greek culture [*Bildung*] is a whole about which it is
impossible to fully understand a part in isolation.

How immeasurable the difficulties attendant upon isolated—perhaps
very small—parts of this great whole are, I pass over in silence. All experts   [78M]
know how much time and effort it often requires just to rectify an incorrect
date, to sort out in a scholarly manner a secondary branch of the legends of the
gods, and to fully work up the entire collected fragments of even just a single
poet.

A complete history of Greek poetry, however, would just not be of
benefit for the scholar alone, and would not simply fill out an important
historical gap for the historian. To me it appears to be also the *essential condition
for the perfection of German taste and art,* which for their part do not assume the
most negligible of positions in our contribution to European culture [*Bildung*].   [207]

Perhaps the first treatise discusses modernity more than the title of this collection would lead one to expect. However, it was only possible to determine the *relation of ancient poetry to modern poetry* and to determine the purpose of the study of classical poetry in general after a not entirely incomplete characterization of modern poetry.

This treatise *on the study of Greek poetry* is only an *invitation* to examine the poetry of antiquity more seriously than previously; an *attempt* (the deficiencies of which no one senses more acutely than I do) to mediate the long-standing dispute of the biased friends of the ancient and modern poets, and to restore peaceful relations in the realm of beauty between natural and artificial culturation [*Bildung*] by means of a sharp distinction; an attempt to demonstrate that the study of Greek poetry is not simply a pardonable hobby but, rather, is and always will be a *necessary duty* of all connoisseurs who bestow genuine love upon beauty, of all critics who want to judge in a universally valid manner, of all thinkers who attempt to determine completely the pure laws of beauty and the eternal nature of art.

I ask that the brief characteristic of Greek poetry contained in this essay not be examined without comparing it to the *outline of a history of Greek poetry,* which will comprise the second volume of this collection. It contains the evidence, the more precise determination, the more extensive exposition of the judgments rendered here.

Adherents of modern poetry will not misinterpret the introduction of the treatise on the study of Greek poetry as my final judgment on modern poetry, and will at least not hasten to the decision that my taste is biased. On [208] the subject of modern poetry I am in earnest;[2] I have loved many modern poets since I was a youth; I have studied many and I believe I know some. Clear-[79M] sighted thinkers will easily guess why I had to choose this position. If there are pure laws of beauty and art, they must be valid without exception. If one takes these pure laws as a standard for the appreciation of modern poetry—without a more *precise determination and a guiding principle for its application*—then the resultant judgment can only be that modern poetry, which almost entirely contradicts those pure laws, is of no value whatsoever. It does not even make claims to objectivity, which is after all the first prerequisite of pure and unconditioned aesthetic value; and its ideal is the *interesting,* that is, subjective aesthetic vitality. Yet this is a judgment that patently contradicts the sentiments! A great deal will have been accomplished if this contradiction is not denied. This is the most direct path to discern the actual character of modern poetry, to explain the necessity of a classical poetry,[3] and finally to be surprised and rewarded by a truly splendid justification of modernity.[4]

If anything can excuse the imperfection of this attempt, then it is the profound *reciprocal influence* between practical philosophy and the history of humanity on the whole as well as in the individual parts. In both sciences there are still immeasurable tracts of land to be *cultivated*. Regardless of which perspective one chooses, there will always be gaps that can only be filled by another perspective. In addition, the spheres of ancient and modern poetry taken together are so large that it is difficult to be at home equally in each field. [209] So that one is perforce nowhere at home. If the basic features and outermost outline are properly established, then every critic—who is not incapable of an overall view of the immense entirety and who is familiar with just a small part of the entire realm—can contribute from his vantage point to a more precise determination and a further exposition.

Schiller's treatise on sentimental poets[5] has—in addition to expanding my insight into the character of the poetry of interest—also cast a new light on the limits of the realm of classical poetry. If I had read it before this essay had been sent to the publisher, the section on the *origin* and the original artificiality of *modern poetry* would have been much less imperfect. To evaluate the last poets of antiquity—as one always has up until now—according to the principles of objective poetry is to judge in a biased and unfair manner. Natural and artificial [80M] aesthetic culturation [*Bildung*] interpenetrate one another and the latecomers of the poetry of antiquity are also the precursors of modern poetry. As faithfully as the *bucolic poets of the Sicilian school*[6] imitated raw nature, so the return of a decadent art to a nature that has been forsaken constitutes the first seed of sentimental poetry. In the Greek idyll the natural is not always represented; rather, the naive is represented, that is, the natural in contrast with the artificial—which only the sentimental poet represents. The more the *idyllic poets of Rome* distance themselves from the faithful imitation of raw nature and [210] approximate the representation of a golden age of innocence, the less ancient they are and the more modern they are. The *satires of Horace* are, in fact, still like those of Lucilius:[7] they are poetic viewpoints on and poetic expressions of Roman urbanity; just as the Doric mimes and the Socratic dialogues are the expression of Doric and Socratic urbanity. Yet some of the original *Roman odes* and *epodes of Horace* (and not the worst!) are *sentimental satires*[8] that present the contrast between reality and the ideal.[9] As Schiller has splendidly observed, the sentimental tone of late Roman satire—which deviated from its original character—is unmistakable in Tacitus and Lucian. The *elegies* of the *Roman Triumvirate*,[10] however, are lyrical and not sentimental. Even in those enchanting poems of Propertius, whose subject matter and spirit are quintessentially Roman, no trace of a reference to the relation between the real and ideal— which is the characteristic trait of sentimental poetry—is to be found. Yet there is in all, especially in Tibillus[11]—just as in the Greek idylls—a longing for a simple rural nature out of antipathy toward the degenerated urban culture. It is extremely surprising that the *Greek eroticists* are thoroughly modern when it comes to the organization of the whole, the tone of the representation, the style of the allegory, and even the grammatical construction. Their principle is not a striving for an unformed subject matter and raw life as such, but a subjective interest in a specific type of life, in an individual material (as is the case in Oppian[12] and much earlier in the Sotadic poems).[13] Compare, for instance, *Achilles Tatius*[14] with an extremely ordinary Italian or Spanish novella. After setting aside the national and coincidental, one will be surprised by the most perfect similarity.

[211]

[81M]

It was remarkable and reassuring for me that in Schiller's splendid characterization of the three sentimental types of poetry the indication of an *interest in the reality* of the ideal is silently presupposed or is patently pointed out in the concept of each of them. Objective poetry, however, has nothing to do with reality. It strives only after a *play* that would be as dignified as the most holy solemnity; it strives after an *appearance* that—as the most unconditioned truth—would be valid and legislative. Precisely because of this, the deception that is necessary to interesting poetry, and the technical truth that is a law of beautiful poetry, are so completely different. You have to at least temporarily *seriously believe* in a Golden Age, in a heaven on earth, if sentimental idylls are to delight you. As soon as you notice that the sentimental satirist is only wallowing in a lugubrious dream or calumny—no matter how much poetic vivacity he has—he can only entertain you; he can no longer seize hold of you and enthuse you.

It is extremely important not to overlook this characteristic trait of interesting poetry, because one will otherwise run the risk of confusing the sentimental with the *lyric*. Not every poetic expression of the striving for the infinite is *sentimental*—only those that are bound up with a reflection on the relation between the ideal and real.[15] If the pure, undetermined striving for the infinite that is fixed to no single object does not remain the prevalent mood of the mind—as in the fragments of *Sappho, Alcaeus, Bacchylides* and *Simonides,* the *Pindaric poems,* and the vast majority of those *Horatian odes* that are modeled after the Greeks and that are not sentimental but rather lyrical— despite all the change of sentiment: then no complete lyrical beauty is possible. The general striving for inner and outer limitation—which so characteristically distinguishes the age of the origin of Greek republicanism and the age of Greek lyric poetry—was the first expression of the invigorated faculty for the infinite. Only in this way did a lyrical disposition become a lyric art, which one cannot deny is the case with *Callinus, Tyrtaeus, Archilochus, Mimnermus,* and *Solon*—even if a sublime mood and elevated beauty is not to be found in their fragments. Not every poetic representation of the absolute[16] is sentimental. In the entire realm of classical poetry the representation of the unmatched *Sophocles* is absolute.[17] The absolute is also presented, for example, in *Aeschylus*

[212]

and *Aristophanes*. The former, although he does not attain his ideal, does provide a living manifestation of infinite unity; the latter, a living manifestation of infinite abundance. The characteristic traits of sentimental poetry are an   [82M] interest in the reality of the ideal, the reflection on the relation between the ideal and real, and the reference to the individual object of the idealizing imagination of the poeticizing subject. Only by means of the *characteristic*, that is, the presentation of the individual, does a sentimental mood become poetry. The *sphere of interesting poetry* is not exhausted by the three kinds of sentimental poetry; and an *analogon of style* could obtain in interesting poetry in accordance   [213] with the relation of the sentimental and characteristic.[18]

According to the opinion of the majority of philosophers, it is a characteristic trait of the *beautiful* that the pleasure taken in it be *uninterested;* and whoever simply admits that the concept of the beautiful is practically and specifically unique—even if he only sets it forth as something problematic— and leaves its validity and practicality undecided, cannot deny this. Beauty is thus not the ideal of modern poetry; it is essentially distinct from the interesting.

In the entire realm of the science of aesthetics the *deduction of the interesting* is perhaps the most difficult and complicated task. The justification of the interesting must precede the explanation of the origin and cause. After the completed natural culturation [*Bildung*] of the ancients decisively decayed and was hopelessly degenerated, a *striving for an infinite reality,* which soon became the general mood of the age, was instigated by the loss of a finite reality and the destruction of a perfected form. One and the same principle produced the colossal excesses of the Romans and—after it saw its hopes disappointed in the world of the senses—the peculiar phenomenon of neo-Platonic philosophy   [214] as well as the general tendency of that remarkable period in which the human spirit seemed to reel toward a universal and metaphysical religion.[19] The decisive moment of Roman moral history—in which people lost the sensibility for that which appears beautiful and that which is morally adroit, and the human race sank down to brute reality—has not gone unnoticed by perceptive historians. It may be demonstrated by means of the most felicitous natural culturation [*Bildung*]—whose capacity for perfection in the long term must necessarily be *limited*—that the *aesthetic imperative* cannot be satisfied perfectly; and that artificial aesthetic culturation [*Bildung*], which can only follow a completely dissipated natural culturation [*Bildung*], must begin there where the former ended—namely, with the interesting. It must pass through many stages before it can attain objectivity and beauty according to the laws of an objective theory and the example of classical poetry: thus it is thereby proven   [83M] that the interesting—as the necessary propaedeutic for the *endless perfectibility* of the aesthetic disposition—is *aesthetically admissible*. For the aesthetic imperative is absolute, and since it can never be fulfilled perfectly, it must at least be ever closer to attaining it through the endless appropriation of artistic development [*Bildung*]. According to this deduction, which founds its own science— *applied poetics*—the *interesting* is that which has provisional aesthetic value. The interesting has indeed necessarily also intellectual or moral content: yet I doubt whether it also has *value*. The good, the true, should be enacted, known, not presented and perceived. I do not put much store by human knowledge that is supposedly created out of Shakespeare, or a virtue created out of [215] Héloïse—despite the praises heaped upon them by those who want to amass testimonials for poetry. Yet the interesting in poetry has always only a *provisional validity*, much as a despotic government.

As dangerous as it is to coin neologisms, it nonetheless seemed to me, and it still seems to me, to be utterly necessary to distinguish the tragedy of Sophocles and Shakespeare—poetic types that are opposed to one another in virtually all their aspects—by means of an important adjective. Yet the designation of philosophical tragedy no longer seems to be the most appropriate. It would perhaps be more fitting to designate that tragedy, the concept of which in pure poetics is deduced a priori (according to the guidance of the categories), and the example of which is provided by the poetic arts of the Greeks—the *objective* tragedy; and, by contrast, to designate the Shakespearean style of poetry, which organizes an absolute, interesting whole out of sentimental and characteristic elements, the *interesting* tragedy. If one furthermore wants to designate as tragedy the poetic style of Corneille, Racine, and Voltaire—out of exaggerated indulgence for the capriciousness of the ordinary turn of phrase: then one could distinguish them by means of the adjective French in order to remind oneself that this is only a national presumption.

An outline of a history of Greek poetry should be followed as directly as possible by a *history of Attic tragedy*.[20] It will not have to determine simply the *highest pinnacle* that classical poetry attained; rather, it must be able to explain in the most clear manner the developmental stages of its history. For, as the Platonic Socrates maintained, ethical perfection is more visible in the larger totality of the state, than in the individual man: thus the developmental laws of Greek art history are—if I may express myself in such a manner—displayed in [216] a larger script in Attic tragedy.

[84M]   If the relation of Greek poetry to modern culture [*Bildung*] as well as Greek culture [*Bildung*] in general is determined, if its development [*Bildung*] in general is determined, if its developmental stages and its types, its boundaries and developmental laws are determined: then the outline and the sketch of the whole is thoroughly mapped out. In the future, this collection will also encompass the development [*Bildung*] of politics.[21]

NOTES

Critical Introduction

1. Xenion, "Die Zwei Fieber." Friedrich Schiller, *Sämtliche Werke*, Vol. 1 (Leipzig: Temple, 1911), p. 319.

2. See Hans Eichner, "The Supposed Influence of Schiller's *Über naive und sentimentalische Dichtung* on F. Schlegel's *Über das Studium der Griechischen Poesie*," *Germanic Review* 30(1955), pp. 260–264. Eichner carefully details how the essay was written in ignorance of Schiller's text, while the preface was clearly written under its influence. For a discussion of the relation of Schlegel's work to Schiller—as well as a thorough analysis of Schlegel's aesthetics—see Leonard P. Wessell, Jr., "The Antinomic Structure of Friedrich Schlegel's 'Romanticism,'" *Studies in Romanticism* 47(1972), pp. 243–258.

3. We should ponder the question Blanchot posed: "Which is the true Schlegel? Is the later the realization of the ealier?" (p. 164). "The Athenaeum," trans. Deborah Esch and Ian Balfour, *Studies in Romanticism* 22(Summer 1983), pp. 163–172. One must also consider to what extent Schlegel presents a full-fledged championing of the ancients in *On the Study of Greek Poetry*. As Raymond Immerwahr notes: "The essay itself, and especially the preface, which was written later, far from being a confident championing of the ancients against the moderns, are an agonized, at times even desperate, effort to reconcile the grandeur of Dante, the beauty, depth, and richness of Shakespeare, and the exciting promise of Goethe, with the ideal of classical harmony achieved by the Greeks" (p. 379). "Classicist Values in the Critical Thought of Friedrich Schlegel," *Journal of English and Germanic Philology* 79(1980), pp. 376–389.

4. As Victor Lange observes: "Few European writers have been so ceaselessly and so brilliantly concerned with the large philosophical assumptions as well as the specific means and purposes of literary criticism as was Friedrich Schlegel, and among them there is none whose achievement is more elusive and more difficult to assess" (289). "Friedrich Schlegel's Literary Criticism," *Comparative Literature* 7.4(1955), pp. 289–305. Geoffrey Hartman has characterized him as a "playboy philosopher." *Criticism in the Wilderness* (New Haven: Yale University Press, 1980), p. 280. Kevin Newmark summarizes the questions criticism often leaves us about Schlegel: "Was Friedrich Schlegel a

serious philosopher or a mere *littérateur,* a dilettante, or worse, a *farceur,* an intellectual practical joker, a pretentiously literate buffoon?" (pp. 905–906). "L'absolu littéraire: Friedrich Schlegel and the Myth of Irony," *MLN* 107(1992), pp. 905–930. For further discussion of these issues, see Marcus Bullock, "Eclipse of the Sun: Mystical Terminology, Revolutionary Method and Ecstatic Prose in Friedrich Schlegel," *MLN* 98(1983), pp. 454–483. Setting off these ruminations was no doubt Wilhelm Dilthey's scathing comment: "His philosophy was dilettantism." *Leben Schleiermachers* (Berlin: de Gruyter, 1970), p. 249. See also Raymond Immerwahr, "The Subjectivity or Objectivity of Friedrich Schlegel's Irony," *Germanic Review* 26(1951), pp. 173–191. This difficulty in assessing Schlegel is not merely confined to the problem of coming to terms with his earlier work. In fact, it is characteristic of the understanding of Schlegel in general.

5. The tacit consensus seems to be that, since Schlegel argued for the prime importance of the fragment, it is acceptable to not even look for any systematic aspect to Schlegel's thought. Instead, one may browse through texts such as the *Fragments* or *Ideas* and take whatever suits one's purposes.

6. It should be pointed out that a great deal of work has helped to make it clear the extent to which the work of the Romantic Schlegel is predicated upon the earlier phase of classicism. Unfortunately, much of this work remains confined to German-speaking scholars of Romanticism. Although many critics rightfully ought to be cited here, I refer the reader to the important work of Ernst Behler, Manfred Frank, and Peter Szondi.

7. Schlegel comments in one of the *Critical Fragments:* "In the ancients we see the perfected letter of all poetry; in the moderns we see its growing spirit." *Philosophical Fragments,* trans. Peter Firchow (Minneapolis: University of Minnesota Press, 1991), p. 11.

8. See Friedrich Schlegel, *Wissenschaft der Europäische Literatur,* ed. Ernst Behler (Paderborn: Ferdinand Schöningh, 1958), pp. 3–188.

9. Friedrich Schlegel, *Geschichte der Alten und Neuen Literatur,* ed. Hans Eichner (Paderborn: Ferdinand Schöningh, 1958), p. 18.

10. Brinkmann rightly points out that this has nothing to do with the imitation of Greek poetry. Rather, what is at stake is the search for a *transcendental principle* of modern poetry (p. 367). "Romantische Dichtungstheorie in Friedrich Schlegels Frühschriften und Schillers Begriffe des Naiven und Sentimentalischen," *Deutsche Vierteljahrsschrift* 32(1958), pp. 344–371.

11. For more extensive treatment of this issue, see Hans Robert Jauss, "Fr. Schlegels und Fr. Schillers Replik of die 'Querelle des Anciens et des Modernes," in Hugo Friedrich and Fritz Schalk, *Europäische Aufklärung. Herbert Diekman zum 60. Geburtstag* (München: Wilhelm Fink, 1967).

12. For further discussion of the "querelle" in France, see Hubert Gillot,

La Querelle des Anciens et des Modernes en France (Paris: Honoré Champion, 1914) and Hippolyte Rigault, *Histoire de la querelle des anciens et des modernes* (Paris: Hachette, 1856). For a concise overview, see Joan DeJean, *Ancients against Moderns: Culture Wars and the Making of a Fin de Siècle* (University of Chicago Press, 1997), pp. 42–66. For an overview of these issues in relation to Germany, see Karl Menges, "Herder and the 'Querelle des Anciens et des Modernes,'" *Eighteenth-Century German Authors and Their Aesthetic Theories: Literature and the Other Arts,* ed. Richard Critchfield and Wulf Kupke (Columbia: Camden House, 1988), pp. 147–183.

13. Behind all these debates that were seemingly restricted to literary criticism lie large-scale philosophical issues. For what is at stake is the very conception of the development and growth of knowledge. The resistance to the abandonment of the ancients as a cultural model is a resistance to the shock of modernity. For the essence of modernity is a mode of culture and knowledge production that acknowledges no model. The ancients, accordingly, have to be surpassed because knowledge progresses, and builds upon and exceeds previous achievements. For most in the eighteenth century this was defined by a vision of progress that was cumulative and linear. Lurking in the German vision of the debate, however, is a more suspicious understanding of the linearity of progress. The sensitivity to the issues of cultural relativism creates a greater awareness of the nonlinearity that revolutions in knowledge and cultural production create.

14. As Raymond Immerwahr notes: "The essay itself, and especially the preface, which was written later, far from being a confident champion of the ancients against the moderns, are an agonized, at times even desperate, effort to reconcile the grandeur of Dante, the beauty, depth, and richness of Shakespeare and the exciting promise of Goethe, with the ideal of classical harmony achieved by the Greeks" (p. 379). Immerwahr, "Classicist Values in the Critical Thought of Friedrich Schlegel," *Journal of English and Germanic Philology* 79(1980): 376–389.

15. This reading of Schlegel was lent considerable authority by two influential essays by Arthur O. Lovejoy published early in the twentieth century—"The Meaning of 'Romantic' in Early German Romanticism" and "Schiller and the Genesis of German Romanticism." Both were collected in *Essays in the History of Ideas* (New York: Putnam, 1960).

16. Certainly the fact that it is impossible to forget that Schlegel is one of the founders of the aesthetics of Romanticism colors the reading of his early work. It may encourage a surprised overreaction to the praise of antiquity. If it were possible to forget the later Schlegel, it would perhaps be possible to see more clearly the extent to which *On the Study of Greek Poetry* is genuinely concerned about modern culture.

17. Brinkmann, "Romantische Dichtungstheorie," p. 353. Peter Szondi

also notes that Schlegel's concern in this essay is the study of the developmental laws of ancient and modern culture and the difference between the two—in other words, a theory of both antiquity and modernity (p. 105). *Poetik und Geschichtsphilosophie.* Vol. 1. (Frankfurt a.M.: Suhrkamp, 1980).

18. As Franz Nobert Mennemeier suggests, "Schlegel does not seek to oppose Greek and modern literature; rather, he seeks to produce a critical, productive reflexion." *Friedrich Schlegels Poesiebegriff Dargestellt anhand der Literaturkritischen Schriften* (Munich: Fink, 1971), pp. 22–23.

19. The pontification and condescension one hears about the last phase of Schlegel's work is the result of people incapable of conceiving of a more heinous act than having the wrong opinion. It is also moral hypocrisy on the part of those incapable of understanding the political complexities of the history of Europe. One wonders what the average American would say, if— because, like Germany, we were an unaffiliated collection of states—a Canadian Napoleon were able to defeat and invade us, dragging many of us off to a futile and fatal campaign against Mexico. Would it be that strange to call for a *United* States of America, so that we might form a more perfect union and ward off a repetition of such events?

20. As Eberhard Huge notes, Schlegel's guiding assumption in the essay is that the presentation of the story of the history of Greek poetry would achieve a theory of beauty. *Poesie und Reflexion in der Aesthetik des frühen Friedrich Schlegel* (Stuttgart: Metzler, 1971), p. 11.

21. Victor Lange: "There exists for Schlegel no categorical distinction between literary criticism and literary history" ("Friedrich Schlegel's Literary Criticism," p. 304).

22. For further discussion, see Walter Jackson Bate, *The Burden of the Past and the English Poet* (Cambridge: Belknap, 1970) and Jochen Schmidt, "Griechenland als Ideal und Utopie bei Winckelmann, Goethe, und Hölderlin," *Hölderlin Jahrbuch* 28(1992–1993), pp. 94–110.

23. As Hans Eichner notes: "its primary reference was chronological, so that it included all poetry written in the European vernacular (as distinct from classical Latin) from the earliest times through and beyond the sixteenth century" (p. 103). Eichner adds: "Until 1797 Friedrich Schlegel employed the phrase exclusively in this sense" (p. 103). "Germany/Romantisch-Romantik-Romantiker," *"Romantic" and Its Cognates. The European History of a Word,* Hans Eichner, ed. (Toronto: U of Toronto P, 1972). See also Eichner's discussion of the term in in "Friedrich Schlegel's Theory of Romantic Poetry," *PMLA* 71(1956), pp. 1018–1041.

24. Clemens Menze observes of this notion: "The basis of the doctrine of *Bildung* is the infinite perfectibility of human nature. The notion of *Bildung,* however, is not tantamount to a form of humanism. For *Bildung* is part of the

self-articulation of the divine." *Der Bildungsbegriff des jungen Schlegels* (Rutingen: Henn, 1964), p. 15.

25. Kathleen Wheeler defines Schlegel's new conception of modernity as a resolution of an earlier antinomy: "Friedrich Schlegel then transformed the original meaning of his term 'romantic' to signify the characteristic synthesis of these pairs of opposites common to all great art, where before 'romantic' had been used merely as a historical term in relation to modern literature" (pp. 7– 8). From this shift, Wheeler argues, Schlegel concludes: "All truly great modern art is close to Greek literature in its essential aesthetic principles" (p. 7). "Introduction." *German Aesthetic and Literary Criticism: The Romantic Ironists and Goethe.* Kathleen Wheeler, ed. (Cambridge: Cambridge University Press, 1984.) However, as Heinz-Dieter Weber suggests, one should not draw hasty parallels: "One cannot speak of an identification of 'Romantic poetry' with the earlier 'interesting poetry' in the sense of a simple reversal. Already in the early studies Schlegel is concerned with a transcendental principle of poetry as well with the conception of a 'dynamic that would extend into the infinite,' in the sense of a progressive universal poetry." *Friedrich Schlegels "Transzendentalpoesie." Untersuchungen zum Funktionswandel der Literaturkritik im 18. Jahrhundert* (Munich: Fink, 1973), p. 141.

26. As Ingrid Oesterele suggests, the dichotomy between antiquity and modernity becomes transformed into a struggle within modernity itself. Thus the issue concerns not antiquity and modernity but modernity and futurity (p. 174). See "Der 'glückliche Anstoß': ästhetischer Revolution und die Anstoßigkeit politischer Revolution. Ein Denk- und Belegversuch zum Zusammenhang von politischer Formveränderung und kultereller Revolution im Studium-*Aufsatz* Friedrich Schlegels" in *Zur Modernität der Romantik,* Dieter Bansch, ed. (Stuttgart: Metzler, 1977), pp. 167–216.

27. For further discussion of the relation between Kant and Schlegel, see Rodolphe Gasché's "Forward: Ideality in Fragmentation," in Friedrich Schlegel, *Philosophical Fragments,* trans. Peter Firchow (Minneapolis: University of Minnesota Press, 1991), vii–xxxii.

28. As Anne K. Mellor notes: "Schlegel thus defines divinity with human consciousness" (p. 73). *English Romantic Irony* (Cambridge: Harvard UP, 1980). While Mellor's study as a whole deals with the English Romantic tradition, the initial chapter, "The Paradigm of Romantic Irony," contains an extended and incisive discussion of Schlegel.

29. In this regard, see Robert S. Leventhal, *The Disciplines of Interpretation. Lessing, Herder, Schlegel and Hermeneutics in Germany, 1750–1800* (New York: Walter de Gruyter, 1994). Leventhal notes: "Schlegel utilizes the notion of 'disinterestedness' in Kant's *Kritik der Urteilskraft* and historicizes it precisely by rendering it the guiding principle of Antiquity" (p. 263).

30. As Ernst Behler notes: "One way of 'fichtesizing' in artistic fashion was pursued by Friedrich Schlegel with his theory of irony. Schlegel's early writings of 1795–1798 on Greek literature already reflect this process. They are dominated by that axiom of transcendental idealism postulating a strong antagonism of nature and human freedom which marks the early phase of idealistic thought as represented by Kant, Schiller, and finally Fichte. Schlegel depicted the entire course of Greek literature as a dramatic exemplification of this process" (p. 59). Ernst Behler, "The Theory of Irony in German Romanticism," in *Romantic Irony,* Frederick Garber, ed. (Budapest: Akadémiai Kiadó, 1988). See also Marike Finlay, *The Romantic Irony of Semiotics: Friedrich Schlegel and the Crisis of Representation* (Berlin: de Gruyter, 1988). As Finlay notes: "Poetry's self-grounding is romantic irony's revolt against philosophical domination, a revolt which takes the basic form of Fichtean transcendence, but which is not the representation of the philosophical ego's extra-discursive transcendence" (pp. 135–136).

31. As Eberhard Huge suggests, Schlegel does not want to dismantle modern principles of understanding; rather, they should be led to their completion (p. 42). *Poesie und Reflexion in der Aesthetik des frühen Friedrich Schlegel* (Stuttgart: Metzler, 1971).

32. Ernst Behler notes with regard to the relation to Hegel: "Historical reality provided him with concrete models and perceptions for the formation of this theory, and one of his most basic convictions was that of a complementary relationship between historical investigations on the one hand and theoretical and systematic ones on the other. As I see it, Schlegel was the first among the idealistic philosophers to develop an historical consciousness out of speculative idealism and to affirm the complementary relationship between history and theory which was later to become the essence of Hegel's philosophy" (p. 58–59). Behler, "Origins of Romantic Aesthetics in Friedrich Schlegel," *Canadian Review of Comparative Literature* (1980), pp. 47–66. For further discussion, see Behler's "Friedrich Schlegel und Hegel," *Hegel-Studien* 2(1963), pp. 203–250.

33. For further discussion of the relation between Schlegel and Fichte, see Kurt Röttgers, "Fichtes Wirkung auf die Frühromantiker, am Beispiel Friedrich Schlegels. Ein Beitrag zur 'Theoriepragmatik,'" *DVLG,* 51(1977), pp. 55–77 and Werner Hamacher, "Der Satz der Gattung: Friedrich Schlegels poetologische Umsetzung von Fichtes unbedingtem Grundsatz," *MLN* 95(1980), pp. 1155–1180. (The latter was published in English in *Premises: Essays in Philosophy and Literature from Kant to Celan,* trans. Peter Fenves (Cambridge: Harvard University Press, 1996).

34. For further discussion of the relation of the cultural debate about modernity to German philosophy, see Walter Jaeschke, "Early German Idealist

Reinterpretations of the Quarrel of the Ancients and Moderns," *CLIO* 12.4(1983), pp. 313–331.

35. Mennemeier suggests that a universal poetry faces art much as the Fichtean ego faces the nonego. *Friedrich Schlegels Poesiebegriff,* p. 324.

36. Timothy Clark notes in relation to this issue: "Consciousness is engaged in a ceaseless transcendence of its finite dimensions, a process undergone as the very movement of reading" (p. 234). "Modern Transformations of German Romanticism: Blanchot and Derrida on the Fragment, the Aphorism and the Archictectural," *Paragraph,* 15.3(1992), pp. 232–247.

37. As Jauss notes: "The perfection of a determination of the pure beauty of ancient *art* became the specific character of a completed *history* of this art" ("Replik," p. 130). In "Vom Wert des Studiums der Griechen und der Römer," Schlegel characterizes antiquity as possessing a cyclical system. Yet history itself is characterized by a system of infinite progress. Thus a natural *Bildung* is a necessary prerequisite for artificial *Bildung,* indeed, for historical progress itself.

38. The contradictory nature of the essay may, in fact, merely indicate the precision of thought at work in it. The essay is part of a larger attempt in German culture to articulate a post-Kantian philosophy by means of cultural history. For a well known and intriguing example, see Heinrich von Kleist's "On the Marionette Theater," trans. Carol Jacobs, *Connecticut Review* 44.1(1997), pp. 49–55.

39. A Roman town destroyed in A.D. 79 along with Pompei by the eruptions of Mt. Vesuvius. It was discovered in 1709. Regular excavations began in 1738. The exploration of the site continued in an unfortunately haphazard and often secretive manner. Winckelmann, who visited the site, was provoked to write a tract denouncing the procedures employed there.

40. Ernst Behler, "The Impact of Classical Antiquity on the Formation of the Romantic Literary Theory of the Schlegel Brothers," in *Classical Models in Literature,* Zoran Konstantinovic, Warren Anderson, and Walter Dietze, eds. (Innsbruck: Amoe, 1981), p. 139.

41. For an overview of the issues surrounding Winckelmann's death, see Lionel Gossman, "Death in Trieste," *Journal of European Studies,* 22(1992), pp. 207–240.

42. Particularly in the German-speaking parts of Europe Shakespeare presented an example of clear achievement in modernity that no longer met the demands and requirements of a literary theory derived from Aristotelian doctrines. Lessing, Herder, Schlegel, and Goethe all worked to establish Shakespeare as a model of modernity. This necessitated in turn the search for an aesthetic theory that would establish the validity of a distinctly modern culture.

Klopstock, Schiller, and Goethe are further, more contemporary, examples of what is aesthetically sound in modernity.

43. Richard Brinkman argues that there is no break between the classicist Schlegel and the Romantic Schlegel. Rather, Schlegel's Romanticism is simply the result of thinking through a problem to its logical conclusion ("Romantische Dichtungstheorie," p. 358). One should also relate these issues to Schlegel's notion of universal poetry. For further discussion of this topic, see Ernst Behler, "Friedrich Schlegels Theorie der Universalpoesie," *Jahrbuch der deutschen Schillergesellschaft*, 1(1957), pp. 211–252.

44. For a further discussion of these issues, see Ernst Behler, "The Impact of Classical Antiquity on the Formation of the Romantic Literary Theory of the Schlegel Brothers," *Classical Models in Literature*, Zoran Konstantinovic, Warren Anderson, and Walter Dietze, eds. (Innsbruck: Amoe, 1981), pp. 139–143.

45. Further discussion of Schlegel's philosophy and aesthetics, see Manfred Frank, *Einführung in die frühromantische Ästhetik* (Frankfurt a.M.: Suhrkamp, 1989).

46. These issues are closely tied to Schlegel's understanding of language. As Winfried Menninghaus notes: "The Romantic discovers the magic, the magical power, of language precisely in its arbitrariness [*"Willkur"*] and instead of being interested in a pre-arbitrary language is interested instead in the post-originary motivational structures of arbitrariness itself" (p. 57). "Die frühromantische Theorie von Zeichen und Metapher," *The German Quarterly* 62.1(1989). See also Menninghaus's *Unendliche Verdoppelung. Die frühromantische Grundlegung der Kunsttheorie im Begriff absoluter Selbstreflexion* (Frankfurt a.M.: Suhrkamp, 1987).

47. Walter Benjamin, *Der Begriff der Kunstkritik in der deutschen Romantik* (Frankfurt a.M.: Suhrkamp, 1973), p. 62.

48. As Walter Benjamin explains: "For the Romantics, criticism is much less the judgment of a work than the method of its completion" (*Kunstkritik*, p. 13).

49. Szondi, p. 116.

50. Ernst Behler, "Einleitung," Friedrich Schlegel, *Über das Studium der Griechischen Poesie*, p. 27.

On the Study of Greek Poetry

1. TN. The word employed by Schlegel for "poetry" is "Poesie." Toward the end of the sixteenth century, *Poesie* was borrowed from the French

poésie, which in turn was derived from the Latin *poesis* and the Greek ποίησις. Originally, it denoted production in general or an activity that produced something. It should be noted that, up until Plato and Aristotle, "poetry" did not exist as a concept in Greek antiquity. It only gradually came to be restricted to things poetic and lyrical. *Poesie* thus referred to that which all the linguistic arts shared and which precisely made them arts. It was seen to be the foundation of the language arts. By the middle of the nineteenth century, *Poesie* began to be replaced with *Lyrik* and *Dichtkunst.* Therefore, while a major focus of Schlegel's essay is a study of Greek poetry from the melic to the Hellenistic lyric, a major concern here is with that which constitutes the foundation and limits of the language arts. To a great extent, Schlegel is simply being faithful to the Greek understanding of poetry. The Greeks did not, as modern critics have tended to do, conflate all of poetry with the personal lyric. Poetry for the Greeks encompassed the epic, dramatic, and lyric. Indeed, according to Dionysius of Halacarnasus, poetry encompassed prose and works of rhetoric as well as philosophy and history. Schlegel continued to remain true to this broader understanding of poetry in his later writings. Thus the "Dialogue on Poetry [*Poesie*]" ranges freely over such seemingly nonlyric subject matters as Aeschylus and *Wilhelm Meister.*

2. TN. Strictly speaking, it is impossible to translate *Bildung.* It can mean: development, formation, education, acculturation, and coming-of-age. All these senses should be kept in mind. *Bildung* acquired its importance as a cultural concept in the second half of the eighteenth century. Although it was linked with the movement to reform and formalize education—in both a strict and broad, cultural sense—the concern with *Bildung* originally emerged out of the strong movement of Pietism in Germany, which emphasized the ongoing and persistent effort required to develop and manifest an inner Godliness. This sense of *Bildung* was soon linked by writers like Herder to a philosophy of history. Thus it came to bind the effort to realize the potential of (that is, the divine plan in) both the individual and humanity with the internal logic of the development of a culture. In this way, the Protean concept of *Bildung* could surface in the discussions of the cultural development of various eras in history, in the story of the coming-of-age of a Wilhelm Meister, and in the elaboration of the idea of the modern university. In certain instances where it seemed that no English word could do justice to the meanings being suggested it has been translated as "culturation." The term "culturation" is meant to play off of "acculturation," which describes the process by which an individual enters into and comes to belong to a culture. By "culturation" I mean to suggest the developmental process by means of which a *culture* produces a different form of culture—out of itself—and comes to belong to it.

3. TN. The following was added in W: "Chapter One. On the current

confused state of modern poetics; and where its purpose is to be found. On the principle of artificiality in the origin and in the evolutionary history—as well as in the characteristic traits—of modern poetry, and on the prevailing philosophical orientation, especially in the tragic art, of the moderns."

4. TN. An allusion to 2 Corinthians 12:7: "And lest I should be exalted above measure through the abundance of the revelations, there was given to me a thorn in the flesh, the messenger of Satan to buffet me, lest I should be exalted above measure."

5. TN. While the use of the word "individual" in this text is consistent with Schlegel's use of the word "individuel," it may nonetheless occasionally sound odd in English. However, one should bear in mind that "individual" in English means not only a unique single entity but also: "Distinguished from others by attributes of its own; marked by a peculiar and striking character" (OED2).

6. TN. An allusion to the story told by Pseudo-Appollodorus of Zeus shaping a cloud into the likeness of Hera in order to fool Ixion who had boasted of enjoying her favors.

7. TN. The preceding was changed as follows in W: "Philosophy loses itself in poetic uncertainty and poetry tends towards a brooding profundity."

8. TN. "Peculiarity" will be used to translate "Eigentümlichkeit." "Characteristic" is doubtless a better translation. However, Schlegel also makes frequent use of the term "charakteristisch," for which "characteristic" is clearly the most appropriate translation. The reader should not associate "peculiarity" with the possible connotation of "strange" or "eccentric." Rather, its original meaning should be kept in mind: a distinctive feature, especially one that belongs primarily to one person, group, or class.

9. TN. The following was inserted at this point in W: "of which only classical examples could lead to the perfection of art."

10. TN. The following was added at this point in W: "assuming one does not seek to inquire into and put forward an entirely different perspective on modern art than that which has previously existed."

11. TN. As usual, Schlegel has in mind an older and broader meaning of the word "costume." The OED2 defines the background to costume as follows: "Used, by Italian artists, of guise or habit in artistic representation, and in this sense adopted in French and English early in the eighteenth century. Thence transferred to manner of dressing, wearing the hair, etc., and in later times to dress." Schlegel also draws on the following meaning the OED2 provides: "The custom and fashion of the time to which a scene or representation belongs; the manner, dress, arms, furniture, and other features proper to the time and locality in which the scene is laid."

12. TN. A reference to a story recounted by Aeschylus about the fifty

daughters of Danaus. Danaus quarreled with his brother Aegyptus over their father's inheritance. In an attempt at compensation, Aegyptus offered to marry the fifty daughters of Danaus to his fifty sons. Danaus, however, fled to Greece with his daughters to become King of Argos. Eventually, Aegyptus' sons found Danaus and laid siege to Argos. As there were no wells in Argos, Danaus feared dying of thirst. Hence Danaus finally relented and accepted Aegyptus' offer. Yet he instructed his daughters to kill their husbands on their wedding nights. For committing this deed, the Danaïds were condemned in Hades to filling jars riddled with holes.

13. TN. Goethe, *Faust: Part One,* 3250–1.

14. TN. The word "revolution" was changed to "rebirth" in W.

15. TN. One should not associate the more recent connotation of catastrophe—namely, a dramatic and disastrous turn for the worse—with Schlegel's use of this word. Catastrophe derives from the Greek, meaning overturning, end, and conclusion. It was the technical term in Greek for the dénouement of a drama, in which the final resolution of the conflict was presented in an overturning and reversal. In this sense, the OED2 defines it as: "An event producing a subversion of the order or system of things."

16. TN. The rest of the sentence was rewritten in W as follows: "all practices and concepts of pagan antiquity."

17. TN. The rest of the sentence was rewritten in W as follows: "communal character of our artificially progressive European culture [*Bildung*] presented from a different and new perspective."

18. TN. The phrase "were the mythology of romantic poetry" was replaced in W with "and Catholic symbols were a rich storeroom and a unique kind of modern mythology for the poetry of the Middle Ages."

19. TN. In W "a total revolution" was replaced with "a great historical transformation."

20. TN. The following was added in W: "and, on the contrary, entrust its poetic vulgarity with a self-satisfied self-consciousness to the everyday artistic fare of commonplace plays and novels."

21. TN. The rest of the sentence was rewritten in W as follows: "seeks the inwardly necessary or the evolution of the external in the apparently coincidental change of the outwardly mutable."

22. Regardless of whether these dominating concepts are obscure and confused, they can and should not be mistaken with the drive as the governing principle of culturation [*Bildung*]. Both are different from one another not according to the degree but the type. In fact, dominating concepts can cause similar propensities and vice versa. Nonetheless, the governing force is unmistakable because both orientations are entirely opposed to one other. The tendency of the entire drive aims for a uncertain goal; the tendency of the

isolating understanding aims for a specific goal. The decisive point is whether the organization of the whole, the orientation of all forces is determined by means of the effort of the whole and yet undivided capacity for striving and feeling, or by means of an individual concept and intention. (TN. This note was incorporated into the text of W.)

23. TN. The following was inserted at this point in W: "according to aims of the understanding or the concepts of reason, the impetus of which."

24. TN. The rest of the sentence was rewritten as follows in W: "a direction that is so wonderful and nonetheless, in comparison with the prototypes of antiquity, merely subjectively beautiful."

25. TN. In W "understanding" was replaced with "the reflective understanding—as the capability to produce ideas—."

26. TN. "Particular organization" was changed to "living personality or an organic characteristic" in W.

27. TN. The following was inserted at this point in W: "One can search for and discover the poetic meaning of these musical syllabic games and these echoes of fantasy only in the most profound characteristic of sensibility. Wherever rhyme does not have any other foundation than surmounted difficulties, the pleasure in an unexpected word, and the outward polish of a meaningless, melodious sound for an ear used to monotony—as is usually the case with truly modern poets—rhyme treated in such a manner must appear as something barbaric and reprehensible."

28. TN. The following was inserted at this point in W: "and enduring in the change of feelings and passions."

29. TN. The following was inserted at this point in W: "and poetically characterize by means of the elements of language."

30. TN. The phrase "artificial universal religion" was replaced in W with "a thoroughly spiritual and universal religion by means of which life in its entirety as well as all art and culture [*Bildung*] became more intellectual."

31. TN. The phrase "entirely national" was replaced in W with "merely national and was still entrusted to the love and evolution of individual peoples until the common essence of it finally proclaimed itself in its generality and stepped forward."

32. TN. The rest of the sentence was rewritten as follows in W: "confusion of all naturally given relations and an absolute uncertainty about its own further determination."

33. TN. The rest of the sentence was rewritten as follows in W: "and eradicate natural free development [*Entfaltung*] in the progression of modern culture [*Bildung*] and art."

34. TN. The following was added in W: "and natural, free evolution in the progression of modern culture [*Bildung*] and art!"

35. TN. In order not to be confused by Schlegel's use of the word "chemical" it is important to disregard the modern concern with the various elements and atomic structure and simply bear in mind the most essential and basic definition of chemistry. As the OED2 neatly defines it: "That branch of physical science and research, which deals with the several elementary substances, or forms of matter, of which all bodies are compound, the laws that regulate the combination of these elements in the formation of compound bodies." From this it is easier to see the sense Schlegel is applying to the consideration of the various histories of poetic production.

36. TN. The following was added in W: "There arise thereby many transitions and intermediary stages, and truly new combinations in poetry, for which there is no concept—indeed, not even an appropriate place in the ordinary theory of art."

37. TN. Much of Schlegel's discussion here is dependent upon some familiarity with the history of the taxonomy of the arts. The Greeks did not restrict the notion of art to the fine arts. Rather, art was characterized by the skill necessary to produce something according to rules. Art had less to do with meeting certain aesthetic criteria of beauty than with craftsmanship and technique. Thus all the crafts, including carpentry and cooking, fall under the rubric of art. Interestingly, poetry was not considered an art as it was not produced according to rules. Plato distinguished between a productive and imitative art. Poetry, accordingly, could be considered an imitative art. Aristotle solidified this classification in the *Poetics* by providing rules for poetry to follow. Schlegel's notion of the representational arts should be understood as being aligned with the imitative arts.

38. TN. The preceding was rewritten as follows in W: "The distinguishing trait of fine art is founded in the free play of the forces of the soul, without a determined goal of the understanding."

39. TN. This sentence was replaced with the following in W: "I consider authentic didactic poetry to be an ideal representation whose ultimate goal and inner spirit is entirely philosophical; in it is to be found the true disclosure about the inner essence of this genre, which appears in our ordinary theories of art as merely an extraneous excrescence and as an exception that is not to be explained; also to be found in it is the disclosure about the position this genre occupies in the totality of intellectual productions."

40. One also speaks of the *pleasurable* arts as a subsidiary form of the fine arts, from which they are separated by an endless chasm. Pleasurable rhetoric is [243] not any more closely related to the poetic arts than any other sensual dexterity that Plato forbade to call art and that he put in the same class as the culinary arts. In the most general sense *art* is every natural or acquired skill used to carry out some purpose of man in nature; it is the skill necessary to make some

theory practical. The goals of men are in part infinite and necessary, in part limited and coincidental. Art is, therefore, either a *free art of ideas* or a *mechanical art* of needs, whose forms are the *useful* and pleasurable arts. The material, within which the law of the mind is disclosed is either the world within man himself or the world outside of him, either the nature that is immediately or mediately bound to him. The free art of ideas breaks down into the *art of life* (whose forms are the *art of ethics* and the *art of the state*) and into representational art, whose definition has already been given. Scientific representation— be its implement arbitrary description or pictorial imitation—distinguishes itself from the representation of art in that it seldom choses and never forms or discovers the subject matter, although it organizes what is at hand according to the laws of the representing spirit. In a word, it is not ideal. The representational arts divide themselves into *three classes,* each according to whether its goal is the truth, beauty, or the good. Both of the first two classes are spoken of in the text. The existence and the specific difference of the third class appear to me undeniable. There are, it seems to me, ideal representations in poetry, whose goal and tendency is neither aesthetic nor philosophical but *moral.* It would not be inconceivable that the imparting of ethical excellence—formerly an integral part of Socratic philosophy that was driven away by Scholasticism—would have taken refuge in poetry. The medium by means of which virtue was disseminated among the Greeks, and which was heightened, intensified, and multiplied by means of intimate, mutual proximity—friendship or masculine [244] love—virtually no longer exists. The ethical artist discovers there only an ideal representation with which to be able to satisfy the inborn artistic drive that belongs to every great master to impart his gift, to plant his spirit in the minds of his students. In individual cases, the boundaries are often very difficult to determine. The decisive point is the *organization of the whole.* The specific structure of a didactic work permits itself least of all to be misjudged. If it is the lawless organization of a beautiful facility, then the work is aesthetic. A free outpouring of ethical feeling, lacking an accommodating polish and a law-governed unity, tends to occur in *moral poetry*—to which I would ascribe certain famous German works instead of to the philosophical class. Hemsterhuys speaks of a philosophy that would be similar to the *dithyramb.* What else could he understand by this than the most free outpouring of ethical sensibility, the imparting of a noble and good ethos. I would term this philosopher's *Simon* to be Socratic poetry. The organization of the whole seems to me at least to be neither didactic, nor dramatic, but rather *dithyrambic.* (TN. Note incorporated into text of W.)

41. TN. The following was added in W: "by means of which among the ancients ultimate beauty in the rhythmic movement of artistic dance was

joined to the merely imitative and passionate or mimetic components of drama to form a complete whole."

42. TN. The following was added in W at this point: "of a nature destroyed in a discordant universe, whose tragic disarray it frightfully mirrors in a faithful image."

43. It was a pleasant surprise for me to see this perfect coherence acknowledged by the judgment of a great writer. Everything that Wilhelm in Goethe's *Meister* says about it and about the character of Ophelia strikes me as particularly apt; his explanation of how Hamlet *became* what he is is truly divine. One should also not forget what he *was*. (TN. This note was revised as follows in W: "This perfect interrelation was acknowledged by the judgment of a great poet. What is said about *Hamlet* and the character of Ophelia as well as all the individual elements of *Hamlet* in Goethe's *Meister* is truly splendid. Yet the idea of the whole, as well as of this genre in general, remains untouched. Namely, the idea of this peculiar tragic world view, which rests upon the soul-piercing, meditative feeling about the eternally unresolvable dissonance of a human existence that has been utterly ruined."

44. The object of drama in general is to manifest a mixture of humanity and fate, and which binds the greatest content with the greatest wit. The interrelation of the particular can be completed into an unconditioned whole in two ways. Humanity and fate are either presented in complete harmony or *in complete strife*. The latter is the case in philosophical tragedy. This mixed appearance, when fate predominates, is termed *an event*. The *object of philosophical tragedy* is thus a tragic event, whose mass and outward form is aesthetic, and whose content and spirit is philosophically interesting. The consciousness of this strife arouses the feeling of *despair*. One should never confuse this ethical pain over infinite lack and indissoluble strife with *animal-like fear*: since the latter (in which the spiritual is so intimately bound up with the sensual) often accompanies the former in man. (TN. Incorporated into the text of W, with the following addition: "It is only in another tragedy of the same writer— namely, *King Lear*—that this tragic element within the awareness of the general disintegration of the world is taken up on a grander scale and executed with a broader scope. In *Hamlet,* however, the essential idea of this peculiar artistic genre is at least presented in a manner that is more understandable and easier to comprehend for most.")

45. TN. The work of Shakespeare served as a rallying point in the struggle for literary modernity in the late eighteenth century in Germany. Already in the *Hamburg Dramaturgy,* G. E. Lessing used Shakespeare to argue against the rigid application of Aristotle's *Poetics* that French Classicism had established. Goethe likewise—from his *Sturm und Drang* period to the end of

his career—championed Shakespeare as a true model of literary form. Goethe's discussion of Shakespeare in *Wilhelm Meister,* in particular, had a great impact on Schlegel. Shakespeare thus functioned not only to help writers resist the Aristotelian unities in drama as followed by the French and promulgated by such critics as Gottsched but also to suggest the range in form, characterization, and style modern literature should attempt to achieve.

46. TN. The following was inserted at this point in W: "according to the standards of antiquity."

47. TN. The preceding was rewritten as follows in W: "His representation is not purely objective; rather, it assumes an entirely individual stamp and peculiar local color; it is entirely taken up in a specific style."

48. TN. The following was added as a new paragraph in W: "One must question whether and how one is to attain in poetry a pure style, objective truth, and the ideal of beauty by means of such an elaborate style. This requires a separate and independent investigation."

49. TN. Schlegel made this paragraph the beginning of chapter 2 in W. He added the following notes: "Chapter Two. Further development and contrast of the interesting with the beautiful. Objections of adversaries about the task of modern poetry and its possible resolution. Of the approximation of objective beauty; and of the possibility of a new rebirth of poetry. Of art's need for a perfect intuition, in addition to theory; how the works of the Greeks present such a prototype."

50. Even where beauty is most loudly proclaimed, one finds upon closer analysis only the interesting. As long as one judges artists not according to the ideal of beauty but according to the concept of *virtuosity, vitality* and *art* remain only two different views of one and the same principle of aesthetic judgment; and the adherents of *correctness* and *genial originality* are distinguished not by virtue of principle, but rather by the tendency of their critique toward the positive or the negative. (TN. This note was incorporated in the text of W.)

51. TN. The following was inserted at this point in W: "poetic being or that which has been newly produced."

52. TN. The rest of the sentence was rewritten as follows in W: "artistic sensibility; and a poetry that has itself become mad takes refuge even in the disgusting."

53. The shocking has three subdivisions: that which revolts the imagination—the *bizarre;* that which outrages the senses—the *disgusting;* and that which torments and tortures the feelings—the *horrible.* This natural evolution of the interesting satisfactorily explains the different paths of the more refined and common art. (TN. This note was incorporated in the text of W. Also added in W to the sentence in the text is the following: "a poetry that has itself become mad takes refuge even in the disgusting.")

54. TN. The rest of the sentence was rewritten as follows in W: "artistic taste grasp that objectivity in the representation of beauty, artistic development [*Bildung*] would remain lasting and established for ever."

55. TN. This sentence was rewritten in W as follows: "Are not all intentional efforts towards this goal of art—when it has not been properly grasped by the understanding—futile?"

56. TN. An allusion to the strength of the model of antiquity both for poetic production and aesthetic theory within Germany. This "obsession to imitate" was fostered in such important works as the *Attempt at a Critical Poetics for the Germans* (1729) by Johann Christoph Gottsched (1700–1766), which held up Aristotle and Horace as models rather than more recent writers like Shakespeare or Milton. This viewpoint had come under increasing attack, particularly by such prominent critics as Lessing and Nicolai.

57. TN. See *The Odyssey*, iv, 456–459:

> First he turned into a great bearded lion,
> and then to a serpent, then to a leopard, then to a great boar,
> and he turned into fluid water, to a tree with towering branches,
> but we held stiffly on to him with enduring spirit.

In this passage, Menelaus recounts to Telemachus how, on his journey home from Troy, he escaped from the island of Pharos. To do this he captured the seagod Proteus, who provided him with the necessary information to return home. The passage quoted recounts the shapes Proteus assumed in his attempt to escape Menelaus.

58. TN. The preceding was rewritten as follows in W: "If the inimical element, which confronts spirit in a constraining manner everywhere in its evolutionary struggle, does not receive support—as in an outward natural catastrophe."

59. TN. It is perhaps worth noting that the word "revolution" in the preceding sentences was removed, in every instance, in W.

60. *The moral healing force* of human nature is, in general, incredibly strong and not entirely dissimilar to the unique organic capabilities of some types of animals whose tenacious life force replaces and reproduces limbs that have been torn off. (TN. This note was incorporated into the text of W.)

61. TN. Despite the importance of Winckelmann in inspiring his study of the Greeks, Schlegel maintains here Lessing's influential assessment of the plastic arts in *Laoköon*.

62. TN. The following was inserted at this point in W: "the music of oratory, is of a far more spiritual type and the root out of which it comes forth and within which it operates."

63. TN. The rest of the sentence was rewritten as follows in W: "the plastic artistic sense for beauty in sculpture and the noble form in the material figure; it is, on the other hand, capable of a limitless perfection and can be reproduced more easily out of the most profound corruption by means of a spiritual rebirth."

64. TN. The rest of the sentence was rewritten as follows in W: "our century of perfected reason."

65. TN. A reference to the contemporary effort to find a natural origin for a national literature. A well-known instance of this effort were the so-called works of Ossian (as he was known in Germany), *Fragments of Ancient Poetry collected in the Highlands of Scotland* (1760) and *Fingal* (1762). In fact, they were—ironically enough—creations of James Macpherson (1736–1796). A complete German translation appeared in 1768–1769. Herder and Goethe in particular received these with enthusiasm. In England, Thomas Percy (1729–1811) helped foster an interest in these issues with the publication of *Reliques of Ancient English Poetry* (1765).

66. TN. This sentence was rewritten as follows in W: "The rule of the interesting, or characteristic, in the content and a peculiar, ingenious, or engaging manner in the methodology, forms a thoroughly heterogeneous artistic law in the poetic arts."

67. TN. The rest of the sentence was rewritten as follows in W: "a general rebirth in the realm of art and beauty."

68. TN. The phrase "aesthetic revolution" was changed in W to "rebirth in fine art."

69. TN. The rest of the sentence was rewritten as follows in W: "the whole of the age and the nation in which the art of beauty is to blossom is nobility of character and an ethically enhanced mood."

70. TN. "Organ" means both instrument and tool and a faculty of the mind or spirit. It was first used and developed by Aristotle as a biological term. As such, it was subordinated to its function; it was a structural part of a larger whole. This understanding of "organ" began to be revised in the late eighteenth century, particularly by J. C. Riel, who emphasized the autonomy of organs. At issue here was the liberation of the organic from the mechanical. The German Idealists, however, repudiated this notion of "organ," arguing that it was a part—a tool—of a larger, organized body. (See Kant, *Critique of Judgment,* §65.) Schelling also denounced the new understanding of organ, arguing that its individuality was derived from the whole.

71. Verum est index sui et falsi," as Spinoza says. (TN: "Truth is the index of itself as well as falsehood." The following sentence was inserted before this sentence in W: "For the true, as it is understood, as it comprehends and

becomes aware of itself, teaches us to recognize above all else error in its uttermost depths as the untruth that stands opposed to it.")

72. TN. A reference to the religious origin of Greek drama. Plays were considered part of the cult of Dionysus and assumed both a religious and civic function.

73. TN. The following was inserted at this point in W: "It requires a separate treatment to determine the degree to which the poets of Greek antiquity represent for us that perfect intuition—in terms of the utmost prototype of beauty in art—according to the different types and developmental stages of art."

74. TN. In W chapter 3 begins at this point, with the following summary: "Chapter Three. Brief outline of the ideal of beauty in the works of the Greek poetic arts, of its classical perfection; of the earliest ages of its initial natural culturation [*Bildung*], up until the subsequent epochs of an already decadent art, through all the stages of the culturation [*Bildung*] of antiquity and the course of its entire evolution as well as its cycle, and how the summit of the utmost in beauty was attained on the pinnacle of the perfected art of tragedy."

75. TN. The rest of the sentence was rewritten as follows in W: "from the general course of the artistic development [*Bildung*] of other peoples."

76. TN. The rest of the sentence was rewritten as follows in W: "let it be understood, worshipfully honored only the liberal abundance of nature, the autonomous force of spirit, and the legitimate harmony of the mind."

77. TN. *The Iliad,* XXIII, 141–153:

He stood apart from the pyre and cut off a lock of fair hair
which he had grown long to give to the river Spercheios, and gazing
in deep distress out over the wine-blue water, he spoke forth:
"Spercheios, it was in vain that Peleus my father vowed to you
that there, when I had won home to the beloved land of my fathers,
I would cut my hair for you and make you a grand and holy
sacrifice of fifty rams consecrate to the waters
of your springs, where is your holy ground and your smoking altar.
So the old man vowed, but you did not accomplish his purpose.
Now, since I do not return to the beloved land of my fathers,
I would give my hair to the keeping of the hero Patrokles."
He spoke, and laid his hair in the hands of his beloved
companion, and stirred in all of them the passion of mourning.

Homer, *The Iliad,* trans. Richmond Lattimore (Chicago: Univeristy of Chicago Press, 1961), p. 454.

78. TN. *The Iliad,* XXIV, 508–516. Achilleus is moved by Priam's impassioned plea for the return of his son Hector's body:

So he spoke, and stirred in the other a passion of grieving
for his own father. He took the old man's hand and pushed him
gently away, and the two remembered, as Priam sat huddled
at the feet of Achilleus and wept close for manslaughtering Hektor
and Achilleus wept now for his own father, now again
for Patroklos. The sound of their mourning moved in the house. Then
when great Achilleus had taken full satisfaction in sorrow
and the passion for it had gone form him mind and body, thereafter
he rose from his chair, and took the old man by the hand, and set him
on his feet again, in pity for the grey head and the grey beard.

(*The Iliad,* p. 488.)

79. *The Iliad,* XXI. TN. The relevant passage (99–113) is as follows:

Poor fool, no longer speak to me of ransom, nor argue it.
In the time before Patrokles came to the day of his destiny
Then it was the way of my heart's choice to be sparing
of the Trojans, and many I took alive and disposed of then.
Now there is not one who can escape death, if the gods send
him against my hands in front of Ilion, not one
of all the Trojans and beyond others the children of Priam.
So, friend, you die also. Why all this clamor about it?
Patrokles also is dead, who was better by far than you are.
Do you not see what a man I am, how huge, how splendid
and born of a great father, and the mother who bore me immortal?
Yet even I have also my death and my strong destiny,
and there shall be a dawn or an afternoon or a noontime
when some man in the fighting will take the life from me also
either with a spear cast or an arrow flown from the bow string.

(*The Iliad,* p. 420–421.)

80. TN. In an epic essentially about the inability to control passions, Diomedes distinguishes himself by the calm and dignity of his demeanor. In Book IV of *The Iliad* Agamemnon ridicules Diomedes for his supposed cowardice. He also states that Diomedes is especially a disappointment given that he is the son of the brave Tydeus. Unlike Achilleus, Diomedes does not respond in kind to Agamemnon's provocation. Later, in Book IX, when Agamemnon despairs of ever achieving victory and urges the Achaians to return home,

Diomedes responds with a reasoned speech urging the Achaians to remain and fight.

81. TN. Winckelmann, *Thoughts on the Imitation of Greek Works in Painting and Sculpture* (1755). The phrase "Edle Einfalt und stille Größe" (noble simplicity and serene grandeur) was a key and well-known phrase from Winckelmann.

82. TN. This sentence was rewritten as follows in W: "Chivalry appears incomparably more homogeneous in the Middle Ages; although, in accordance with its idea, a rich blossoming of fantasy grew out of it and lives in its element; yet in the course of the development of life in its entirety it has less natural strength and is confined more to a specific, ethically compulsory form."

83. TN. In W the phrase "Compare them with those representations" was replaced with "Compare these in and of themselves quite marvelous and alluring products of fantasy with those classical depictions of heroes."

84. TN. In W the phrase "so truly human" was replaced with "already in that earliest of ages emerged entirely out the idea of beauty and is at the same time genuine."

85. TN. The phrase "by the result of such a *philosophical deduction*" was replaced in W with "by the philosophically acknowledged foundation of everything particular within the one idea and within the essence of the whole."

86. TN. Appolonius Rhodius. Schlegel refers here to the various adventures in the *Argonautica*. The *Argonautica* was very popular and was adopted by Theocritus, Varro of Atax, and Virgil. According to later judgment, the *Argonautica* lacks consistent unity and is marred by a zealousness to demonstrate learning. His love of etiology is one clear indication of this. Thus, Schlegel implies, the *Argonautica* contains elements of the greatness of Greek poetry in fragmentary form, but on the whole it demonstrates the decay of Greek poetry in the Hellenistic period.

87. TN. The rest of the sentence was rewritten in W as follows: "ultimate, unsurpassable and no longer to be surmounted boundary of what is proximately attainable, which is the perfection that is unattainable and merely conceivable as idea."

88. TN. The following was added in W: "that is, the divine or the eternal."

89. I must plead for permission to set forth these and a few other fundamental principles and concepts problematically for the sake of context. I will not be remiss in providing the proof of these in what follows. (TN. This note was incorporated into the text of W in the following form: "We allow ourselves—by reason of context—to put to use these fundamental principles and concepts of the immutable, totality, of the harmoniously organized unity, and of the endless abundance of life, as just so many elements and organic

components of everything good, divine, and beautiful; since in what follows there will be more frequent opportunities for further explication.")

90. In individual types of art technical accuracy can—as in pure tragedy or pure comedy—call for an ideal divergence from that which in actuality is true and probable. (TN. Incorporated into the text of W at the end of the sentence.)

91. TN. In W the following was inserted at this point: "at least in the initial stage."

92. TN. The rest of the sentence was rewritten as follows in W: "of the utmost completion and flowering of art such as is attained in culture [*Bildung*] and by means of the unfettered evolution of nature, but it can never completely reproduce that harmonious symmetry."

93. TN. The rest of the sentence was rewritten as follows in W: "is entirely a construction of the human spirit, and consequently capable of infinite perfectibility, as well as limitless decay."

94. TN. Timoleon, Greek general and statesman of the fourth century B.C. Timoleon was renowned for his bravery and skill in military ventures. He coupled this with a remarkable sense of modesty and patriotism. In a military campaign, he defended the Syracusans from the Cartheginian tyrants. His patriotism and hatred of tyrants was so great that he helped to carry out the murder of his own brother—for whom he had earlier risked his life to defend—in order to prevent him from reinstating despotism.

95. TN. In W "a technical world" was replaced with "a self-sufficient art-world of representation."

96. TN. Polycleitos (c. 450–c.415 B.C.) was a Greek sculptor. The statue Schlegel refers to, the Doryphoros or "Spearbearer," is known to us through Roman copies. The most complete copy is from the Herculaneum. Because the Doryphoros seemed to embody perfectly the very ideal of the human form it came to be known as the "canon." According already to Pliny the Elder, other artists referred to the Doryphoros as the "Canon" and derived fundamental artistic principles from it.

97. TN. As other critics have noted—and as is explicitly evident in this sentence—Schlegel anticipates Nietzsche's discussion of the Dionysian and Apollonian aspects of Greek tragedy in *The Birth of Tragedy*.

98. TN. In W "the existing sketches" was replaced with "the sketches of the characters and events of old legends."

99. TN. Sophocles's *Electra* is indebted to Aeschylus' Oresteia. However, Sophocles reworked the material in a significant manner. Most important, he rearranged the key events of the plot. Instead of ending with the murder of Clytemnestra, the play begins with her murder; Aegisthus is killed later. Thus the most troubling murder is dispatched with quite early.

100. TN. *Philoctetes,* one of the last extant plays of Sophocles. The story was adopted by Aeschylus and Euripedes as well. The play is set during the Trojan war. The Greek Philoctetes was bit by a snake and developed a wound that would not heal. Because of the grotesqueness of the wound and his suffering, he was abandoned by his fellow Greeks on the island of Lemnos. Later the Greeks learn that they will only win the Trojan war with the help of Philoctetes and his bow. The Greeks must then return for Philoctetes and persuade him to help them.

101. In poems the moderns fumble around in the dark after what is unconditionally necessary as well as after the true nature and the precise limits of ethical beauty to such an extent that they have long struggled over the meaning of the simple edict of Aristotle: "The morals in a poem should be good, that is, beautiful." In all of modern poetry the character of Brutus in Shakespeare's *Caesar* is perhaps the sole example of ethical beauty that would not be unworthy of Sophocles. (TN. The last sentence of this note was rewritten as follows in W: "The modern writer draws his moral lessons from a mass of ugly—albeit perhaps utterly faithfully represented—characters and events; while in the representation of antiquity the idea of beauty—as the gentle, external reflection of the inner ethical perfection—is already to be found within the character.")

102. TN. This sentence was replaced with the following one in W: "With regard to the classical in art and in the style of treatment, the entire mass and the development of the evolution of ancient poetry throughout all its phases, genres, and epoches sets forth everywhere through all works an abundance and plenteous surfeit of refined and remarkable elements.

103. TN. The rest of the sentence was rewritten as follows in W: "striving of everything peculiar—and particularly in the spirit of the poet as well as in his words—aims always towards the objectively beautiful."

104. TN. In W this sentence was replaced with the following: "Only in rhetoric did a different situation obtain; there art was truly carried out in accordance with theory and was acquired. Apart from this, however, in all of Greek intellectual culture, and especially in poetry, the unfettered drive, and not the understanding, was, in its striving for complete intellectual development, not only the motive but also the *guiding principle* of Greek culture [*Bildung*]."

105. TN. The next section begins as follows in W: "Chapter Four. Objections against Greek poetry; especially because of its ethical blemishes and deficiencies. Attempt at laying the foundation for a complete theory of the ugly and artistically repugnant in all its varieties, as a contrast to the idea of beauty in art. Response to and consideration of these sketches and errors." Chapter 4 begins with the following section in W: "After we have considered Hellenic

poetry—in its prototypical excellence and in its more unfettered natural evolution—as a complete and perfect artistic intuition for all poetry, we must turn our gaze to the opposing side, and take into consideration all limitations that obtain here, the deficiencies that are found in the Greek poets or that they are usually accused of, as well as the objections in general that are made against their perfection and examine and reply in accordance with a strict comparison to the correct idea of art."

106. Like the characters of Dionysus and Demos in the *Frogs* and *Knights* of Aristophanes. (TN. Incorporated into text of W. In the *Frogs* Dionysus sets out to visit the underworld in order to talk to the great playwrights. Once in the underworld, he pretends to be Heracles. Yet when it becomes apparent that, as Heracles, he is to be threatened with various punishments, Dionysus quickly reverts to being himself. In order to safeguard himself, he changes places with his slave Xanthias. *The Knights* concerns the cynical struggle of slaves to usurp their tyrannical master Demos. Demos (the people) is portrayed as a master that is easily fooled and cajoled by his own slaves).

107. TN. The rest of the sentence was rewritten as follows in W: "and the arbitrary principle of such polemics that misjudge and distort the beauty of antiquity, which are the ubiquitous foundation of modern thought and yet which are seldom articulated very clearly."

108. TN. In W the last word is changed and the following was added: "opposites that can only be discovered, properly understood, and apprehended in their essence as such—one by means of the other. The error lies in the fact that all artistic reproaches are pronounced in accordance with rules, which are applied to individual cases without raising themselves to the level of the universal idea, and which for the most part, moreover, are taken up in an arbitrary manner. Or it occurs according to a vague feeling that is often merely idiosyncratic. One does not go back to the fundamental concept about that which can in general be reproachable in art. Yet clearly such a fundamental concept of the ugly and unformed—as the pure opposite of the idea of beauty—would be utterly necessary for perfect clarity and certainty in artistic judgment."

109. TN. This sentence was replaced with the following one in W: "A positive bad is not opposed to a positive good, although the will—which desires negation and which negates everything else outside of itself—can in other respects also be termed a positive bad; rather, the bad—considered in general and in relation to being—is simply a mere negation of pure or spiritual existence and its essential components, spiritual totality and multiplicity."

110. Even *animalistic play*, in which we humanly sense a more free pleasure, is perhaps only the appeasement of a need—a discharge of superfluous power. Only the *presentiment of what is set against* it can give life its first impetus to rouse and determine its power, to love similar life forms and to hate

the exotic. A being could not even achieve, much less desire, consciousness (which presupposes multiplicity and diversity, and yet which would not be possible in the case of a perfect uniformity) without a presentiment of an enemy; it would persist forever in a lethargic torpor. Fear of extermination is the actual source of animal being. Animalistic fear is only a modification of human fear. Only man, on the other hand, is patently capable of *hope.* (TN. Incorporated into text in W.)

111. TN. The rest of the sentence was rewritten as follows in W: "as a vain virtuoso only strives after the utmost skillfulness in order to astonish thereby by means of wonderment, by means of affectation in other words, and which then occupies the place of true art."

112. TN. Sextus Propertius (c. 50–15 B.C.) was considered the greatest of the Roman elegiac poets. He published four books of elegies, in which the vicissitudes of his love for Cynthia figure prominently. His elegies were remarkable for their intense concentration on the personal and individual. He had announced in the beginning of Book III of his poems his desire to write in the manner of Callimachus and Philetas. For the most part this ambition manifested itself in style and form. His writing was characterized by an allusiveness designed to appeal to a select circle of cognoscenti. Propertius' comments as well as those of others indicate that Callimachus and Philetas were considered the founders of elegiac poetry, yet unfortunately little of their elegiac verse has survived. While perhaps too self-indulgent for the Romans, he attracted the attention of Goethe as well as the Italian poets Petrarch, Tasso, and Ariosto.

113. TN. Callimachus (c. 310–c. 240 B.C.). The only extant works of Callimachus are the *Hymns* and *Epigrams.* His most lengthy and well-known work—of which only fragments remain—was the *Causes* (*Aitia*). It was divided into four books of elegiacs. Thus we are left to conjecture as to the exact nature of Callimachus' contribution to the development of the elegy. From the prologue we can gather that Callimachus emphasized an intimate, small scale that was opposed to the anonymity of the epic. As in the case of Propertius, Callimachus was often referred to or invoked as the founder and precursor of the elegy.

114. TN. Philetas (fourth century B.C.). It has been conjectured—based upon inferences drawn from existing fragments—that Philetas helped to invent the personal love elegy that was fully developed in Propertius. This notion was given credence by Quintilian ranking him as second only to Callimachus as an elegist. In addition, Propertius and Ovid point to Philetas as their model in the production of elegies.

115. TN. The rest of the sentence was rewritten as follows in W: "many works of antiquity were at one time smashed to pieces in a false pious agitation about the undisguised nakedness of these phenomena; a more educated and

more sensible Christian posterity did in no way condone such a destruction of refined art objects, nor did it carry on in a similar manner."

116. TN. This sentence continues as follows in W: "and it has already been often noted that this false delicacy of an affected and brooding nit-picking decorum easily arouses suspicion, or offends, and is exaggerated to the point of unnaturalness, the deeper the corruption is rooted in the customs—and in the imagination itself—and has eaten away at everything."

117. TN. The Fourth Homeric Hymn relates the story of the invention of the lyre by Mercury. The son of Zeus and Maia, Mercury left the cradle on the morning of his birth. He then invented the lyre and stole the cattle of Apollo. To placate the enraged Apollo, Mercury gave him the lyre. Apollo was so delighted with the lyre that he forgave Mercury. The poem has been loosely translated by Shelley.

118. TN. While popular, Euripedes was widely seen to be responsible, together with Socrates, for the spread of impiety in Athens. As a result, only five of his plays were victorious at the Dionysiac festivals. Aristophanes satirized him mercilessly. Suits were brought against him for impiety and dishonesty. The inhospitibility of Athens is generally taken to be the cause of his accepting the invitation of King Archelaus to reside at Pella, the Macedonian capital, at the advanced age of seventy-two.

119. TN. Cinesias was a fifth-century Athenian poet. For various reasons he raised the ire of his contemporaries. He was reputed to be atheistic, effeminate, and a sophist. He was also known for his thin and sickly appearance. Aristophanes employs Cinesias in a comic scene of sexual frustration in *Lysistrata*. Cinesias also appears in *The Birds,* where he is mocked as a lyric poet. Plato also abuses Cinesias in *Gorgias* (501e) for producing lyrics meant to please and not to inform.

120. TN. In W the phrase "are not unrestrictedly free" was replaced with "may not freely unfold themselves within the limits of law-governed order."

121. TN. The following was inserted at this point in W: "in the sense of fair antiquity."

122. TN. The following was inserted at this point in W: "Unrestrained in his language and in his depictions, he is, by his own nature, constantly a defender and eulogist of venerable traditional morals and ancestral customs; and the reckless boldness with which he attacks shameful demagogues and rabble-rousers, precisely before this people, must be acknowledged as a great republican *civic* virtue."

123. TN. The rest of the sentence was rewritten as follows in W: "appearing to gloss over crimes, in that he allows the persons involved in the action to speak in accordance with their passion and their character."

124. TN. The following was inserted at this point in W: "if it otherwise

is conceived and composed in a truly artistic fashion, and if we focus on the art within and do not concern ourselves with the aforementioned unethical aspect."

125. TN. The rest of the sentence was rewritten as follows in W: "entire human, ethical-bourgeois, scientific-intellectual, and poetic-artistic culture."

126. TN. The following was inserted at this point in W: "goodness as well as beauty are both founded upon truth, and it is only an error and delusion if one believes it is possible to tear apart out of this divine triad—and subordinate one to the other—that which could only in the complexity and isolation of individual existence appear separated and contentious—both in its entirety and in its very essence."

127. TN. In W the phrase "a maximum of artificiality" was replaced with "simply a perfected artificiality and an artistic perfection that is fundamentally impossible, that is, utterly unartistically conceived."

128. TN. The rest of the sentence was rewritten as follows in W: "transitory and differs according to time and place and primarily according to the then prevailing level of historical development [*Bildung*]."

129. TN. In W "motivated and it must strive to" was replaced with the following: "well based in the course of the action and should, in as much as the truth of the representation and the peculiar character and emotional state of the speaker allows it."

130. TN. This sentence is rewritten as follows in W: "The realm of God is not of this world; this is also true with regard to the art of beauty, which is at home in our world, mixed as it is out of the spiritual and sensual; such a realm of the invisible lies beyond the horizon of art and would be only an empty shadow lacking spirit and vigor in this world of poetry and appearance."

131. TN. The following section was added at this point in W: "The modern Catholic poet should not search for the peculiar Christian beauty of his poetry in things or in an external environment and historical circumstance—and even less in individual doctrines of faith and truths borrowed from the fountainhead of the divine in order to resolve thereby and fill out what remains incomplete in his poetry; rather, he should search only in the inner transfiguration of a more spiritual and entirely divine beauty—the idea of which can be made concrete even in a (historically considered) non-Christian material. To an even greater extent the poet of antiquity must derive the ethical balance and ethical harmony in his works only from the inner ethical vigor and disposition as well as from the sublimity of character. He must not resolve and decide all at once from on high the riddle of the world and the fate of humanity; for he was endowed only with an abundance of beautiful presentiments about his mythological world instead of clear faith and higher morality. And such a presentiment of faith within sentiments turns up as the

greatest flowering of the soul of genuine poetry in Pindar and Sophocles. Moreover, one should not expect or demand Christian perfection and beauty of temperament from heathen poets. They render and depict for us the perfected sensibility for nature that is replete with life and completely developed powers—in a manner that is, among their better writers, in accordance with ethical order and unity as well as with that essential form of beauty of which Greek art became and always will remain the great prototype."

132. TN. The following was added to the beginning of this section in W: "Chapter Five. Of the mistakes and errors in the imitation of the poetry of antiquity, and of the difficulties that lie in the path of the modern poet. Resolution of the whole; of the rebirth of modern poetry, especially with regard to Germany." The following was added to the text in W: "After we have deliberated, examined, and answered or explained in a uncontentious manner that which appears to be morally deficient or offensive in the poetry of the Greeks to the modern artistic judgment, all that remains is to consider more clearly, and to attempt to resolve one by one, the difficulties that stand in the way of the requisite appropriation and imitation of the poetic arts of antiquity, as well as the objections that one tends to make against it."

133. TN. Theognis (544–c. 480 B.C.). Many of Theognis' poems seek to lecture about the threat of the lower classes who can support a tyrant to overthrow the aristocracy. Thus much of his verse sought to instruct his own city of Megara in the virtues of moderation and traditional values. He was also known for his gnomic verse.

134. TN. Gnomes are moral aphorisms or proverbs. They were present in Greek literature from the time of Homer onward. Gnomes were gradually collected into anthologies (gnomologies) for the purpose of instructing the young. They remained popular through the Middle Ages.

135. TN. In W the phrase "could become childish with age" was replaced with "strives to return in its aging decay with renewed fondness to its earlier mythical age as to the memories of childhood."

136. TN. The following was inserted at this point in W: "and truly bring it back to life—as Klopstock, who attempted it with bold élan in lyric poems in the style of antiquity."

137. TN. Tasso's *Gerusalemme liberata* (1575) strove to present a classical epic in the context of chivalrous romance. As Schlegel suggests, Tasso rejected the loose, episodic style of Ariosto and sought to construct an epic characterized by unity and uniformity of structure and subject matter. In this he was very much an Aristotelian. Thus Schlegel suggests that Tassso was attempting to resurrect the epic within the context of modernity.

138. TN. Luigi Pulci (1432–1484) was a poet of the Tuscan group best known for his chivalrous epic *Morgante* (1478). The epic tells the story of the

paladin Orlando, who is banished from the court of Charlemagne by the plottings of the treacherous Gano. After Orlando successfully battles the pagans in Spain, Gano succeeds in arranging to have Orlando ambushed and killed. Only then does Charlemagne realize the true worth of Orlando and the treachery of Gano. Despite the indebtedness of the poem to the French *chansons de geste*, it is characterized by buffoonery and Rabelesian wit. The poem takes its title from a minor character, a humorous giant who becomes Orlando's squire. Interestingly, Pulci won the admiration of Byron, who found inspiration in him for his own *Beppo, Don Juan,* and *A Vision of Judgment*. What attracted Byron no doubt was not only the *ottava rima* form but also the jesting comic style.

139. TN. Niccolò Forteguerri (1674 -1735) made a name for himself by recasting one of the stories from the *Furioso* in his *Ricciardetto,* which was prevailingly comic in character. Interestingly, Forteguerri attracted the attention of Shelley, who found inspiration in him for his own "The Witch of Atlas."

140. TN. This sentence was replaced with the following in W: "Such a thorough admixture of irony in romantic poetry—from the earliest beginnings to the most recent times of decadence—is certainly no coincidence."

141. TN. The latter half of the *cinquecento* became increasingly concerned with literary theory and criticism. Tasso shared this concern and took great care to insure that his work did not meet with critical disapproval. Upon completing the *Liberta,* Tasso spent two years corresponding with Scipione Gonzaga and other artists, going over in considerable detail various aspects of the poem. Tasso went over questions of form and style; he also considered religious issues as well as factors that might affect popular appeal.

142. TN. This sentence was rewritten as follows in W: "How much did Tasso—who nonetheless strove after a classical notion as he understood it based upon the models of antiquity and the artistic theory that had been handed down—still fortunately retain from romantic costume and fantasy all that did not correspond to the demands of modern artistic judgment with regard to a well-ordered heroic poem."

143. TN. From Horace, *Epistles,* I. 10. 24: "you can expel nature with a pitchfork, but it will still come back. "

144. TN. This sentence was replaced with the following one in W: "It was and remained even until now impossible for the most persistent art to breath an ancient soul and a beautiful artistic form into the modern complex of world and history." The following section was added at this point in W: "There no doubt is a wealth of great poetic beauties and a great abundance of wonderful fantasy in modern heroic legends and poetry; yet everything is disjointed and isolated, like non-contiguous aigulle, and only rarely, and as an individual exception, has a single one of these fragments of these magnificent ancient

poems achieved such a beautiful form and perfection as the German *Nibelungenlied.* Strictly self-contained, the Nordic *Edda*—which harkens from heathen primordial times—stands alone. It stands as if separated by a great chasm from the Gothic heroic songs of the German tribes of the beginning of the Christian era; and it is, at the least, without direct, living contact with a concurrently thriving poetry, although the connecting joints of the former [336]   interrelation can be discovered and demonstrated after the fact by scholarly research. The chivalrous poetry of the actual Middle Ages likewise remained utterly foreign to the ancient heroic epics of the Gothic Age. Indeed, they appear as the spiritual flowering of a new age, which is for the most part hostile and opposed to that ancient heroism; none of them attained such a perfected beautiful form as the German *Nibelungenlied.* Other fragments of heroic poetry, of the chivalrous peoples of the Occident, remained right from the outset only scattered echoes of beautiful legends—isolated romances. They were isolated from one another and without contact with those greater epic cycles. Those poets who, like Dante, founded their elaborate works—which were part of a new great poetry—on Christian symbols, holy legends, and profound allegory, stand again entirely separated and isolated from popular legend in an infinitely elaborate form that has, however, still not progressed to clarity and perfection. Those, however, who, like Tasso and Camoëns, attempt in the context of the general development [*Bildung*] of a flourishing poetry to shape a great, historical and yet still fantastic object more according to the form of the ancients—and who do so actually for no reason and only because they follow the modern trend toward fragmentation—confront for the most part as hostile opponents the older chivalrous songs; they are, moreover, hampered by the artistic form of the ancients they have adopted and are diverted from their goal; they are hindered by this more than anything else from attaining a peculiarly beautiful form of epic poetry that would be appropriate to their modern age and their Christian heroic legends; just as these earlier, at least now and then, had spontaneously evolved in an incomparably better and more felicitous manner without the art of antiquity.

Because the epic legend and poetry of the moderns have remained scattered in an isolated way, incomplete and often also informal, parody took root and established itself quite early within it so that this has become one of its most peculiar traits."

145. Not so much in the energy, as in the material, costume, and the organs. Thus tragedians were composers of satyric drama and never comedians. (TN. Incorporated into text in W.)

146. TN. Although the exact nature of the origin of Greek drama remains obscure, it is known that the Dorians laid claim to the invention of drama in both its tragic and comedic variants. (See Aristotle, *Poetics,* 1448a.) A

secular form of Dorian comedy that lacked a chorus can, accordingly, be seen to have laid the foundation for writers like Aristophanes, Cratinus, and Eupolis. These were usually brief farces or mimes of everyday life.

147. TN. A lost work of antiquity. It was ascribed by Aristotle to Homer. Aristotle maintained that the *Margites* held the same relation to comedy that the *Iliad* did to tragedy. (*Poetics,* 48b–49a.)

148. TN. Pratinas (c. 300 B.C.), Greek dramatist. He is known as one of the earliest tragedians after Thespis. Some thirty-two satyr plays—of which he is believed to be the originator—were attributed to him. Aristotle thought that the satyr drama was a precursor to tragedy.

149. TN. Tragedians usually submitted a satyr play to be performed with their tragedies. Thus Schlegel conjectures that, had we a satyr play from Aeschylus, we would possess a standard by which to judge such plays.

150. TN. Sophron (c. 400 B.C.), writer of mimes. He is credited with lending literary quality to the mime. He thus provided a foundation for Theocritus and Rhinthon. One of the existing manuscripts makes it clear that quotations from Sophron were used by later scholars to demonstrate the nature of the Doric dialect.

151. TN. Rhinthon (c. 300 B.C.), Greek comic playwright. His specialty was the *hilarotragoidia* ("merry tragedy"). These were farces that took as their subject matter tragic themes. The existing plays of Rhinthon suggested that he parodied Euripedes in particular. The plays were also usually bawdy in nature, with the actors employing masks, enormous phalli, and padded stomachs and buttocks.

152. TN. A reference presumably to Ariosto's five comedies. They drew their inspiration from Roman comedy, yet clearly were oriented to contemporary life.

153. TN. The eight of the muses, presiding over comedy and idyllic poetry.

154. TN. *Romans d'aventure* were popular from the twelfth to fifteenth centuries. They were meant to be read and not recited or sung. They often dealt with Arthurian legend, yet focused on the adventures of a hero, which usually included a love story. Unlike other medieval romances, they eschewed magic and supernatural events. For these reasons, the *romans d'aventure* are seen to be a precursor to the modern novel. Around the sixteenth century, the *romans d'aventure* evolved into the picaresque novel. An early—and influential—manifestation of this form was the anonymous *Lazarillo de Tormes* (1554). The picaresque novel flourished in Spain as well as in other parts of Europe. Examples include Le Sage's *Gil Blas* (1715–1735), Grimmelshausen's *Der abenteurliche Simplicissimus* (1669), Defoe's *Moll Flanders* (1722) and *Colonel Jack* (1772), and Fielding's *Jonathan Wild* (1743). Thus Schlegel's suggestion is that the desire to

transform the *romans d'aventure* into a tragic epic was frustrated by the irresistible tendency toward the mock-heroic.

155. TN. This sentence was rewritten after the colon as follows in W: "by renouncing the natural joyousness and the irony intrinsic to their type of poetry, they transformed themselves into farce in their solemn earnestness and have thus—without knowing it or suspecting it—reverted back to that unavoidable irony."

156. TN. The following was added in W: "The meaning cannot be oriented toward beautiful form; indeed, there is not even the physical time to pay heed to the harmonious organization and unity, when all spiritual force—in the conception as well as the representation—is entirely absorbed by the abundance of details in the mass of a historically rich material that is difficult to overlook."

157. TN. The following was inserted at this point in W: "Yet there are exceptions, where nature breaks through the otherwise universal dissipation of the great poetic talents of our modern age and asserts itself in its most essential force and strength."

158. Plato, *The Republic*, Book III. TN. (395a–b.) Socrates here, in a discussion with Adimantus, argues against both the ability and desirability of poets to be both tragedians and comedians. The reason for this is that "the same man is not able to imitate many things as well as he can one" (III, 394e). Socrates concludes from the example of the poet that the guardians should only imitate what is appropriate to them.

159. TN. The following was inserted at this point in W: "All poets who strive in a modern material after the beautiful form of the ancients will have to struggle with great difficulties, and will leave much to be desired in their imperfections. Especially in the noble genres of art, where the idea that comprises the foundation has become something altogether different than it was with the ancients, so that one has only retained the name for an entirely different style and type of poetry. Thus the striving for the old form where the essence has been altered remains, in fact, futile; it leads one astray in a variety of ways. It would have to come to a living fusion—which is in itself no doubt possible—in order to reunify both elements and to secure for Christian beauty in poetry a different mode of that perfection of art and that elevated form evident in antiquity. Without such a fusion and a truly new revival and transfiguration of fantasy, the essential and correct artistic form will remain simply something assumed. Moreover, the idea of it is rarely clearly comprehended but, rather, is always confused with merely coincidental local truths."

160. TN. The following was inserted at this point in W: "Other genres of Hellenistic poetry are already by their very nature and in themselves entirely local. They are not true types of poetry but rather only severed elements of it; or

rather not universally valid types but only types that are based on a particular circumstance."

161. TN. The following was added in W: "There is actually nothing more unnatural than an imitated popular poetry, a feigned natural poetry."

162. TN. Johann Heinrich Voss (1751–1826) was associated with the group known as the *Göttinger Hain* (Göttingen Grove). In 1781 he published an acclaimed translation of the *Odyssey* into German. He also translated Virgil, Ovid, Horace, and Hesiod. What distinguished Voss as a translator was a poetic sensibility coupled with a profound philological knowledge. Indeed, Voß was essentially a philologist before it was even a discipline. His translations served to enrich the German language by the revival of archaic words and the coining of neologisms.

163. TN. The following was added in W: "for spirit—the classical spirit as well as one's own—will certainly escape the strained rhythmic artistic clutches in which the goal of a complete homogeneity none the less remains unattainable."

164. TN. Friedrich Gottlieb Klopstock (1724–1803). Klopstock was a champion of the critics Bodmer and Breitinger, who sought to challenge the authority of Gottsched. In 1748 he published the first three cantos of *The Messiah*, which opened up a new vista for poetry and poetics in Germany. In it, Klopstock rejected the Alexandrine, which was held up as the ideal verse form by French Classicism. Instead, Klopstock took up the hexameter in imitation of Homer and Vergil. This was one of the first noteworthy attempts to write in classical meter in Germany. Although he sought later only to distance himself from it, his emphasis on sensibility and subjectivity is generally regarded as a harbinger of Romanticism.

165. TN. The following was added in W: "It especially consists in being compressed to the same degree of brevity, or where possible, being even somewhat more abbreviated. This venerable old master of German style and art appeared to lay a great worth upon this. The independent poet announces himself—even in the curiosities of expression—in Klopstock's fragments. In Voss's style and manner the rhythmic art displaces everything else."

166. TN. The following was added in W: "Since this time A. W. Schlegel has enriched rhythmic art in that he has, entirely in the manner of the ancients, avoided all trochees in the elegiac poem. It is hard to imagine that this could also be carried out in a longer epic poem."

167. TN. Aristotle addresses this issue in *Poetics* (1459b33–1460a5). Aristotle argues that epic verse found its appropriate verse form in the hexameter, for it is the slowest and weightiest of all verses. Iambic trimeter and trochaic tetrameter, however, lend themselves to movement.

168. TN. The following was added at this point in W: "By means of the

outward form and the letter we will never attain the spirit of the ancients, since we are neither capable of escaping ourselves nor of re-creating our own nature and our language; however, where the spirit has been comprehended and understood, there the inner beautiful form is simultaneously discovered and attained."

169. TN. The following was added in W: "The essence of the art of antiquity—as well as its contrast to modern poetry—consists neither in the outward form and the style of the language of antiquity adopted, nor the so-called classical expression, nor in arbitrary rules and merely coincidental traits but, rather, in the spirit and inner idea of beauty."

170. TN. Marcus Brutus recruited Horace to serve as *tribunus militum* in the Republican army in the battle of Philippi. Despite Schlegel's suggestion, one should not forget Horace's own self-deprecating assessment of his part in the battle. See *Odes* II, vii. Indeed, with his light-hearted mention of dropping his shield in flight, Horace recalls Archilochus.

171. TN. Richard Hurd (1720–1808), Lord Bishop of Worcester and literary critic. The passage is from "Introduction: On Epistolary Writing," which introduces *Epistola ad pisones: With an English Commentary and Notes.* See *The Works of Richard Hurd* (London: Cadell and Davies, 1811), vol. 1, p. 13.

172. TN. Dionysius of Halicarnassus (first century B.C. Greek writer), whose essays on rhetoric and composition sought to lead to a revival of a purer Attic prose in Augustan Rome.

173. TN. The word "exoteric" occurs first in Lucian, who claims that Aristotle himself categorized his own work into the "esoteric" and "exoteric." Hence the OED2 defines it as: "Of philosophical doctrines, treatises, modes of speech, etc.: Designed for or suitable to the generality of disciples, etc.: Belonging to the outer circle; not admitted to the esoteric teaching."

174. TN. The following was inserted at this point in W: "political, in the ancient sense of the word, where it encompasses not merely the state and the communal life of the citizenry and its institutions, but also ethics and life in its entirety in addition to art and the legends about the gods, indeed, even the forms of worship."

175. TN. Book VIII of the *Politics* is chiefly concerned with the role of education in the state. Aristotle argues that education should be a public affair and that it should be governed by laws. He argues for the necessary place of the arts—particularly music and poetry—in education. (See especially his discussion of poetry, painting, and the plastic arts, 1340a–1340b.)

176. TN. Marcus Fabius Quintilianus (c. A.D. 35–c. 100). In A.D. 96 Quintilian published *The Education of the Orator.* Consisting of twelve books, it sought to provide a comprehensive educational and training program for rhetoricians. In the tenth book he surveys a range of Greek and Latin authors.

It is clear here that the predominant criterion is their usefulness in the instruction of rhetoric.

177. TN. The *Epistles* offer an intimate insight into Horace the poet. They are often clearly written in reaction to a specific motivation. None the less, critics are for the most art unclear as to the specific nature of the motivation. In *Epistles,* I. 7, for instance, Horace proclaims his autonomy from his patron, Maecenas. Yet, despite a specific motivation being suggested here, it is unclear exactly what incident triggered this reaction.

178. TN. The rest of the sentence was rewritten as follows in W: "decree so much that has not yet been proven—at any time—by either the spirit that governs and guides history or the historical evolution of humanity itself."

179. TN. The rest of the sentence was rewritten as follows in W: "traces of this are evident in theory, in imitation, in art and its products as well as in the feelings that it encompasses."

180. TN. In W "important revolution of aesthetic development" is replaced with "great rebirth of artistic development."

181. TN. The following was added at this point in W: "and recent changes in the course of human development."

182. TN. In W the phrase "the *dogmatic system of rational and empirical aesthetics*" was replaced with "a purely ideal and merely empirical doctrine of art."

183. TN. In W "*aesthetic judgment*" was replaced with "ideal judgment and all fundamental concepts of art and beauty."

184. See Fichte's *Lectures on the Vocation of the Scholar.* (TN. Note removed in W.)

185. TN. In W "postulates of the aesthetic revolution" was replaced with "conditions for the rebirth of art and poetry."

186. TN. The translation of this phrase does not capture the Kantian overtone of the German: "Der stolzen Vernunft des reinen Denkens."

187. TN. The first three sentences of this paragraph were reworked as follows in W: "The French, however, have in the last century surpassed other nations, and especially the German nation, in the talent necessary for all this by means of the undivided type and nature of their knowledge, by means of their customs, and their inclination to communicate all perspectives and sentiments—for every ruling opinion has always been established in this manner. Precisely because of this they have striven especially to attain a high level of perfection—and believed themselves to have attained—only in public poetry. In that genre of poetry—namely, dramatic poetry—they have turned entirely toward rhetoric. The reason and motivation for this prevalent tendency towards the rhetorical side of art is to be found in the whole form of their social life as well as in political events. However, the same motivations and

circumstances—which in general promote the prevailing tendency towards mere rhetoric in the individual and more profound characters who elevate themselves above this sphere, just as every extreme naturally calls forth its opposite—can provoke an ardor of a higher order, which then proclaims itself as all the more truly poetic and lyric with a spiritual clarity and vigor of expression that one would not expect."

188. TN. The rest of the sentence was rewritten as follows in W: "as soon as great events also arouse great sentiments and opinions, which are expressed lyrically—even if they cannot correspond to the public morals and inclination of the people—yet which, nonetheless, as the more refined soul of the nation, lend a public voice to the more noble aspirations of the few who are more sensitive."

189. TN. The following was added in W: "Nevertheless, the French base their pretensions in poetry merely on that false image of passionate rhetoric, not on their genuinely poetic disposition, which they themselves usually misconstrue."

190. TN. The following was added in W: "Indeed, the earlier German system of art contained merely the initial basis upon which the endlessly diverse and rich studies of modern philosophy evolved and propagated themselves throughout all branches of intellectual development. Nevertheless, these initial attempts at a more profound, incisive theory of beauty have already advanced far ahead of the other nations who have yet to catch up with it."

191. TN. The following was added in W: "and by means of an exceptional gift for historical divination, a profoundly perceptive characteristic and an empathetic imagination that artistically comprehends and that imitates everything—in every manner and form—he laid the initial foundation and sketched out the traits to the new mode of criticism that emerged as the most peculiar fruit out of both German intellectual culture [*Geistesbildung*] and science. Above all, Winckelmann must be named and praised as the one who first lent a new foundation to the history of art and precisely thereby to the [365] science of antiquity. For only through the knowledge of art will the understanding of antiquity be accessible to us, for their culture [*Bildung*] was based entirely on the idea of beauty. According to the doctrine of Plato, correct insight and artistic wisdom emerges out of admiration, that is, out of a profoundly felt, unadulterated enthusiasm for the divine and the beautiful. This was the noble motivation and animating force out of which everything in Winckelmann emerged and by means of which he produced works about art that themselves—as solidly structured works of art and works of the science of history—bore the imprint of immortal permanence. This was also acknowledged by all nations. Before all others, Winckelmann demonstrated and described what a history of art should be: the initial beginnings and seeds; the

higher stages of exposition; the structure and parts of the whole; the types, styles, and schools; the faithful observations and careful evaluation of all of this; the pure insight of the spirit constantly directed toward the idea of the highest beauty. Winckelmann, moreover, did this in the grand style in his history as an expert in art who possessed his own artistic sense. Although his undertaking was directed toward the plastic arts, the application of it towards poetry and the entire intellectual and ethical development [*Bildung*] of antiquity—according to the same noble sensibility for beauty and great artistic wisdom—can be discovered all the more easily and brought to general recognition on the basis of this secure foundation."

192. TN. This sentence was replaced with the following in W: "Since *Schiller* gave it greater vigor of thought and greater verve of passion? One could indeed expect a new spring, a beautiful dawn from such a fertile time, where even the initial efforts—in the midst of a still raw, for the most part disadvantageous, environment—were already so laudably advanced?"

193. TN. Gottfried August Bürger (1747–1794). Bürger was one of the initial poets in eighteenth-century Germany to turn against the authority of the ancients and French classicism. He is best known for the ballads "Lenore" and "The Wild Huntsman." Bürger imbued the popular folk ballad form with a complexity and gravitas hitherto unseen in German poetry. In contrast to Schlegel's praise, it is worth noting that Bürger came in for scathing and damaging criticism at the hands of Schiller in 1791. Schiller refuted Bürger's claim to be a popular national poet, asserting that his poems were immature and unrefined.

194. TN. In W the English were added as important rivals.

195. TN. The following was added in W: "And if they ever were able to comprehend him, they would attempt to acquaint themselves with everything—from the tragic melancholy of his initial, still youthful imagination—other than the pure artistic sense for the beauty of antiquity."

Appendix: Preface

1. TN. See Aristotle, *Poetics* (38–51b1). "Thus the difference between the historian and the poet is not in their utterances being in verse or prose (it would be quite possible for Herodotus' work to be translated into verse, and it would not be any the less a history with verse than it is without it)."

2. TN. The preceding clause was replaced with the following in W: "My aim is not only the approbation of ancient poetry but also just as much the perfection and inner idea of modern poetry."

3. TN. The following was added at this point in W: "for the complete progression of the development of art in its entirety."

4. TN. The following was added at this point in W: "in that one understands the actual idea of it in its proper place and in the context of the whole."

5. In the twelfth section of the *Horen* 95. Also to some extent in the discussion in the eleventh section and in the first section of 96. Here is not the place to examine the author's division of poetry into naive and sentimental, the application of this division to ancient and modern poetry, and the objectivity of interesting art judgment. (TN. The last sentence was removed in W.)

6. TN. Bucolic poetry, which we would term pastoral, found expression in Sicily from the fourth century to third century B.C. The most well-known Sicilian poet—who actually lived most of his life on Cos and in Alexandria—was Theocritus.

7. TN. Gauis Lucilius, Latin satirical poet of the second century B.C. Very little of his work survives. Widely admired in his time, he is credited with defining the notion of satire as a broad form of poetry that included not only invective but also commentary on morals, politics, and literature. In the verse that survives, Lucilius addresses prominent social and political figures as well as highly literate topics.

8. TN. The following was added at this point in W: "in the Schillerian sense of the word."

9. TN. Satirical elements are to be found in both the *Odes* and *Epodes*. The second epode, for instance, illustrates Schlegel's point nicely. It sings the praises of country life only to reveal in the last four lines that the preceding has been the speech of a money-lending townsman.

10. TN. Following the death of Caesar, Octavian, Antony, and Lepidus formed the Triumvirate (42 B.C.). Octavian soon stripped Lepidus of power (36 B.C.). Octavian and Antony ruled as Triumvars until Octavian defeated Antony at Actium (31 B.C.). Elegists of this time include Propertius, Tibullus, and Gallus.

11. TN. Albius Tibullus, Roman poet (c. 50–19 B.C.). Continuing in the tradition of Gallus, Tibullus' elegies focus on his love for a single woman, Delia. Tibullus writes longingly of the simple pleasures of country life. The notion of retiring to the country with his beloved represents an ideal in his poetry.

12. TN. Oppian, Greek writer of the third century A.D. Author of didactic works.

13. TN. Sotades, Greek poet of the third century B.C. Little of his work survives. Sotades was involved in the Hellenistic revival of the use of iambic for invective. He invented a meter and used it to parody the *Iliad,* among other

things. In particular, he is noted for the scurrility and obscenity of his verse. Thus his poem entitled *Priapus* helped to create a special obscene poetic genre, the *Priapeia.*

14. TN. Achilles Tatius, Greek novelist of the second century A.D. His main work was *Leucippe and Clitophon,* a romance of adventure that was long popular and was influential in the development of the European novel. Tatius combined a naturalization of classical events and themes with a predilection toward the fantastic and improbable.

15. TN. The following was inserted at this point in W: "This relation may be thought of as a felicitous agreement—as in the idyllic poems; as a hostile conflict—as in satire; or as a state hovering between unsatisfied longing and melancholic memory—as in the elegy."

16. TN. In W "absolute" was replaced with "infinite and in its way unconditioned and unconditionally perfect."

17. TN. In W "absolute" was replaced with "unconditioned or infinite."

18. TN. The following was added in W: "by means of the strict purity of the sentimental relation as the ruling emotional idea, and by means of the abundance of characteristic truth. For the former, Petrarch may serve as an example; for the latter, however, Shakespeare may serve as an example."

19. TN. In W the phrase "seemed to reel toward a universal and metaphysical religion" was replaced with "reeled into the infinite and seemed to lose itself in a universal and metaphysical faith."

20. TN. In W this sentence was replaced with the following: "The best commentary for this theory and the entire artistic viewpoint in the following treatise would be provided by a history of Attic tragedy carried out entirely in this sense."

21. TN. This sentence was removed in W.

INDEX